ANTHROPOLOGICAL PAPERS OF
THE UNIVERSITY OF ARIZONA
NUMBER 67

Salado Archaeology of the Upper Gila, New Mexico

Stephen H. Lekson

Contributions by
> **Timothy C. Klinger**
> **William B. Gillespie**

THE UNIVERSITY OF ARIZONA PRESS
TUCSON
2002

About the Author

STEPHEN H. LEKSON is Curator of Anthropology at the University Museum, University of Colorado, Boulder. He received his doctoral degree from the University of New Mexico in 1988 and was President of the Crow Canyon Archaeological Center from 1992 to 1995. He has directed field research in the Mimbres, Jornada, Hohokam, Chaco, Mesa Verde, and Rio Grande regions of the Southwest. Although most of his work deals with matters local to those areas, his research interests sometimes consider large scale history and process in the Greater Southwest.

Cover: Four Gila Polychrome vessels and a Chupadero Black-on-white pitcher found in association on a room floor at Dutch Ruin, along with a Tucson Polychrome bowl and a red-slipped corrugated jar (*see* p. 18 and Figs. 2.15, 2.16, and 2.19). Design and graphic by Arthur J. Jelinek, Professor Emeritus, Department of Anthropology, University of Arizona, Tucson.

Frontispiece. Vessels found in association beneath a room floor at Dutch Ruin (Context D, Table 2.6, p. 18). *Top* (clockwise from top right, scale 40%): Chupadero Black-on-white pitcher, Gila Polychrome bowl, Ramos Polychrome jar, and Gila Polychrome bowl. *Bottom* (scale 56%), front and side views of a Ramos Polychrome effigy jar of a kneeling man, apparently smoking a pipe. Design and graphic by Arthur J. Jelinek.

THE UNIVERSITY OF ARIZONA PRESS

This book was set in 10.7/12 CG Times

∞ This book is printed on acid-free, archival-quality paper.
Manufactured in the United States of America.

2004 03 02   4 3 2 1

Library of Congress Cataloging-in-Publication Data

Lekson, Stephen H.
  Salado archaeology of the Upper Gila, New Mexico / Stephen H. Lekson.
    p. cm. -- (Anthropological papers of the University of Arizona ;
no. 67)
Includes bibliographic references and index.
  ISBN 0-8165-2222-7 (pbk. : alk. paper)
  1. Salado culture--Gila River Valley (N.M. and Ariz.) 2. Salado culture--New Mexico--Mogollon Mountains. 3. Excavations (Archaeology)--Gila River Valley (N.M. and Ariz.) 4. Gila River Valley (N.M. and Ariz.)--Antiquities. 5. Mogollon Mountains (N.M.)--Antiquities. I Title. II. Series.

E99.S47 L45 2002
979.1'701--dc21
                            2001008556

Contents

FIGURES

TABLES

Preface

This report began, I suppose, with the excavation of the Villareal II site in 1973 and the survey of the Redrock Valley in 1974. In other ways, it began with a rejected NEH proposal to analyze and publish the Ormand Ruin in 1991. In still other ways, it began with a study of the Dutch Ruin collections at the Johnson-Humrickhouse Museum in 1998. But in its proximate form, it began with the publication of a report on Ormand (Wallace 1998) and Ben Nelson's summary remarks on my chapter in an edited volume on Salado (Nelson 2000). None of those "beginnings" were directly related, but cumulatively they suggested that publication of information on the Salado derived from the Dutch Ruin and Villareal II might be of some use to Southwestern archaeology. The information is intriguing, and I hope that my arguments based on it will be of at least transitory interest.

The data are inherently valuable, but they are far from perfect. The Dutch Ruin was excavated by inspired amateurs, and the surviving records are much less precise than we might wish. Villareal II excavations were, for their time, state-of-the-art: we screened, we used a grid. Today, alas, Villareal II would not past muster for acceptable Cultural Resource Management (CRM) mitigation work. But both the Dutch and Villareal sites, flawed as they are, have things to say, things to tell us. Old damaged data still are data. They may not give us the certainty of shiny new data, but how often do shiny new data give us certainty?

This report presents the Salado of the Upper Gila River region as a group of sites and as a research issue, and introduces two previously unreported or underreported sites: Dutch Ruin and Villareal II. I describe the Dutch Ruin and its remarkable whole-vessel collection in Chapter 2, present a brief review of comparable whole-vessel collections, and summarize the dating of this complex site. After discussing the Villareal II site, its excavation, its collections, and its dating (Chapter 3), I review Upper Gila Salado settlement patterns and ceramic issues, principally but not exclusively from typological perspectives, to provide contexts for the Dutch Ruin and Villareal II settlements (Chapter 4). In the concluding chapter I use the information presented to evaluate the competing models of Upper Gila Salado that have been proposed by archaeologists. Brief summaries of other sites tested in the Villareal II vicinity appear in Appendix A and descriptions of the Villareal II lithic collections are in Appendix B.

Acknowledgments

A number of individuals have contributed mightily to information gathered herein; all are innocent of the arguments. In no particular order, these kind colleagues include: at the Johnson-Humrickhouse Museum, Midge Derby (director), Sharon Buxton (registrar), Patti Malenke, and Phyllis Cotterman, who all greatly facilitated my work with the Dutch Ruin collections; Darrell Creel and LaVerne Herrington, who provided copies of Dutch Ruin photos; Matt Lukovsky, for his work with Dutch Ruin digital images; Lex Lindsay, who initially pointed me to the Dutch Ruin collections and advised me on Maverick Mountain Polychrome and Tucson Polychrome pottery; Patricia Crown, for ceramic counsel; Dr. Shi-kui Wu and Barbara Romig, for shell identifications; Joel Tyberg, for his analysis of the Solomonsville site; Roger Moore, co-director of the Redrock survey, and the Redrock crew (Lynda Anderson, Jennifer Lezac, Chuck Mobley, Christie Williams); Timothy C. Klinger, co-director of the Villareal II excavations, and the Villareal crew (Linda Brown, Liz Horenstein, Ken Robbie, Betsy Skinner).

The various analyses of Villareal II collections were undertaken by Timothy Klinger (ceramics), Betsy Skinner (lithics), William Gillespie (faunal), and Mollie Toll (flotation). Charles M. Mobley analyzed the Redrock survey ceramics. Preliminary editorial assistance was provided by Chris Ward, Devin White, and Catherine M. Cameron, all of the University of Colorado. At the University of Arizona, Carol Gifford undertook the chore of editing the manuscript, Arthur J. Jelinek crafted the cover and frontispiece, and María Nieves Zedeño translated the Resumen. The comments of reviewers Andrew Duff and James Bayman improved the text. To all these friends and colleagues: thanks!

Color is an essential characteristic of archaeological sites and objects, and particularly of pottery. Journals such as *Antiquity* and *American Antiquity* recognize the importance of color illustrations, but few books can afford them. With the support of an anonymous donor, the University of Arizona Press includes a color frontispiece. For increasing the scientific value of this book, I thank the Press and I particularly honor the donor.

When I was young and foolish and just starting out in Southwestern archaeology, I set myself some goals. I wasn't interested in tenure or a GS–9 or even a steady job (I was *really* young and *really* foolish). What I wanted to do was this: to work in the Anasazi, Mogollon, and Hohokam regions and to write useful books in each of those areas. Specifically, I wanted to write about Chaco, Mimbres, and Salado, the Glamour Kids of the Ancient Southwest. More importantly, these three seemed to be the interesting "problems" in Southwestern archaeology. Today, I'd add pre-Classic Hohokam; but Chaco, Mimbres, and Salado were on my original list of "things to do." I have written a few books and articles, but I am particularly proud of my slim contributions to the *Anthropological Papers of the University of Arizona*. There are three, one in each area. "Mimbres Archaeology of the Upper Gila, New Mexico" was published as *Anthropological Paper* 53; my chapter "Great!" was included in John Kantner and Nancy Mahoney's "Great House Communities Across the Chacoan Landscape" (*Anthropological Paper* 64); and now "Salado Archaeology of the Upper Gila, New Mexico" forms *Anthropological Paper* 67. My Chacoan contribution was not a monograph, but I'm older now and I'll settle for what I can get: that's the cycle.

Carol Gifford's dedication to the *Anthropological Papers* has produced an outstanding series of monographs. I am pleased to be in their (and her) company.

CHAPTER ONE

Archaeological History

The term "Salado" refers to a fourteenth and early fifteenth-century ceramic horizon, defined by archaeologists, that stretches across the Sonoran and Chihuahuan deserts of the southern Southwest. It has emerged in the last fifteen years as a major research theme of Southwestern archaeology, but still there appears to be no real consensus on what Salado was (Dean 2000). Villareal II and the Dutch Ruin, two sites in the Upper Gila region of southwestern New Mexico, were excavated about 30 years ago, but information from them is relevant and, I hope, useful for contemporary questions about Salado and the ancient history of the Southwest.

What is Salado? The question might better be asked: What *was* Salado? Fifty years ago, Salado was vital and robust, a force to contend with: Harold Gladwin and Emil Haury saw Salado as a great folk movement, spilling out of the Mogollon Uplands to conquer (or at least co-habit) the deserts of southern Arizona: "when the spearhead of the Salado migration reached the Hohokam villages" (Gladwin 1957: 253). That seminal view of Gladwin and Haury was challenged, amended, modified, and diluted until, by the 1990s, Salado had become a local elite, or a regional cult, or simply a trade ware (for reviews of Salado, see Dean 2000; Doyel and Haury 1976; Lange and Germick 1992). Migration was shunned, but never entirely abandoned (Reid 1989); it has returned to interpretive favor, but its role is now downsized to a modest domain, within the Salado "heartland" of the Tonto Basin northeast of Phoenix, Arizona (Elson, Stark, and Gregory 2000; Reid and Whittlesey 1997: 230–258; but see Clark 2001).

The Salado of Gladwin and Haury was bigger than the Tonto Basin; it engulfed the entire Hohokam region of the Sonoran Desert and extended well into the deserts of New Mexico and northern Chihuahua. In those outer Chihuahuan reaches, Salado escaped the critique and deflation of the Hohokam Salado as expressed by archaeologists. Salado in Chihuahua, in particular, is remarkable for its sharp contrast and clear definition (Lekson 1992a, 2000). When Arizona Salado headed to-

ward archaeological oblivion, partisans could point to Chihuahuan desert sites, and particularly to the Upper Gila, to validate the beleaguered Salado (Doyel and Haury 1976). Yet recently, even in these two regions, archaeologists are localizing the origins of Salado and reducing the range of Salado migrations from the vast vision of Gladwin and Haury to far smaller and contained scales (Nelson and Anyon 1996; Wallace 1998).

Salado of the Upper Gila is ripe for restudy. There have been a surprising number of Salado sites excavated, but most of those excavations took place in the 1960s and 1970s. Unfortunately, most of the major Upper Gila Salado collections (from a half-dozen sites excavated by avocational archaeologists) are now, for various reasons, unavailable. One of the most important Salado collections came from the Ormand Site, excavated in the 1960s; a full report has been produced by Wallace (1998). A major collection from Solomonsville (called Buena Vista, or Pueblo Viejo) in the Safford Valley was also recently analyzed and reported (Tyberg 2000). In this volume I present information from two large Upper Gila Salado collections that do survive, Dutch Ruin and Villareal II.

Salado archaeology of the Upper Gila is a thing of shreds and patches: hobby digs, private parks, highway salvage, field schools, and shoe-string research projects. This is not the best way to know a key region at a critical time period, but it will have to do. The Upper Gila holds a position of particular, if peripheral, importance in Salado studies and the region does indeed tell us about Salado origins and the remarkable fourteenth- and fifteenth-century history of the southern Southwest. More than that, Salado of the Upper Gila offers a case study in archaeological continuity and discontinuity, in both material culture and paradigmatic conceits.

Salado began and remains a pottery phenomenon, tied closely or even exclusively to the Salado polychromes: Pinto, Gila, and Tonto. They are the threads that run through Salado's history and, in the end, they represent the only consensus definition of Salado (Crown 1994; Nelson and LeBlanc 1986). Beyond that pottery

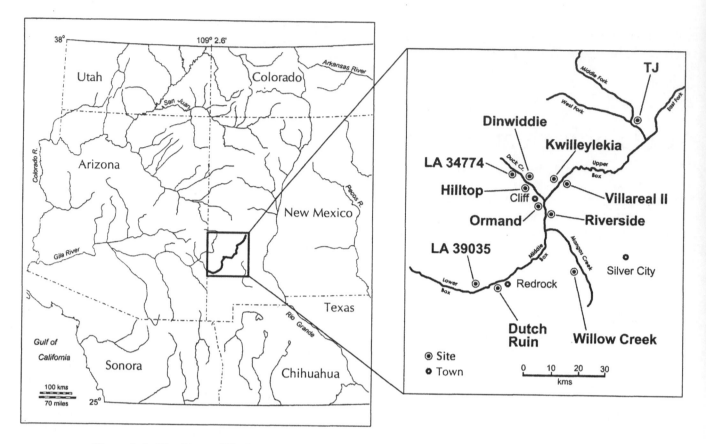

Figure 1.1. The Upper Gila River region and major Salado sites in the Upper Gila River valley.

lowest-common-denominator, archaeologists have proposed a wide range of more detailed models, reconstructions, and ideas. For the cultural taxonomy and historical derivation of Upper Gila Salado, these models fall into four groups: (1) Upper Gila Salado derives from Paquime (Nelson and LeBlanc 1986), (2) it derives from the Mogollon Highlands (Lindsay and Jennings 1968; Wallace 1998), (3) it was a local in situ cultural evolution within the Upper Gila area (Crary and others 2001; Fitting and others 1982), and (4) it was a regional in situ development within the area today encompassed by southwestern New Mexico (Nelson and Anyon 1996). These models are described at greater length in Chapter 5, wherein I propose that the second model, deriving Upper Gila Salado from the Mogollon Uplands, appears to best fit the data.

GEOGRAPHY OF THE UPPER GILA

The Gila River (Fig. 1.1) originates in the Mogollon Highlands of southwestern New Mexico and twists through the long, mountainous Upper Box to the Cliff Valley, where it dramatically leaves the mountains and

flows into an oasis that is 20 km long and 2 km wide (12.4 by 1.2 miles). The Cliff Valley has huge agricultural potential, realized both in pre-Contact and in modern times. At the lower end of the Cliff Valley, the river enters the Middle Box, another long defile that contains a few isolated pockets of arable land. The Middle Box separates the Cliff Valley from the Redrock Valley, a second agricultural oasis about 16 kms (10 miles) long, but narrower than Cliff Valley. Redrock, too, was (and is) extensively farmed. The Redrock Valley ends at the Lower Box, a short (10-km, 6.2-mile) narrows that opens up again just above the towns of Virden and Duncan. The Duncan-Virden segment of the Gila River is heavily farmed, an astonishingly bright green line in the sand when viewed from the Albuquerque-Tucson airplane, and it should be rich with archaeology, but that archaeology is essentially unknown (Lekson 1992a). Below the Duncan-Virden Valley, the Gila River flows through another short narrows and then into the Sonoran desert and the archaeologically better-known Safford Valley.

The Mogollon Mountains at the upper end of Cliff Valley rise to almost 3,300 m (9,843 feet). Pine forests loom above the Chihuahuan desert grasslands. The lower end of Redrock Valley is technically Chihuahuan desert, but many elements of Sonoran desert flora and fauna sneak in. The Cliff and Redrock valleys are bordered by gravel-capped terraces and peneplains that support desert grasslands; the river bottoms are rich riparian environments, with permanent water, gallery forests, and (today) extensive diversion irrigation systems. In both valleys, the riparian environments have been significantly altered by intensive agriculture and introduced species.

The geology of the entire region is predominantly volcanic, with massive ash deposits of rhyolite and andesite forming the most visible exposures. The mountains surrounding both valleys are heavily mineralized, with several deposits of significance to ancient populations. In the upper reaches of Mangas Creek (a tributary of the Gila in the Cliff Valley) are the White Signal turquoise deposits (Lekson 1992a) and in the upper Redrock Valley there is a large exposure of ricolite serpentine; both were mined in pre-Columbian times.

THE UPPER GILA AFTER
A.D. 1000

The archaeological history of the Upper Gila parallels that of southwestern New Mexico (Fig. 1.2), with a Late Pit House period (A.D. 500–900) of large pit house villages with great kivas, followed by the somewhat controversial, transitional Mangas phase (900–1000) and thereafter, the celebrated Mimbres phase (1000–1150; Anyon, Gilman, and LeBlanc 1981; Lekson 1999a). These early time periods are described in several additional reports (Lekson 1990a, 1992a; Woosley and McIntyre 1996), and for good short summaries of the larger region of which the Upper Gila was a part, see Fish and Fish (1994) and Hegmon and others (1999) or a longer treatment by Lekson (1992a). A brief overview of the post–A.D. 1000 Upper Gila sequence is offered here.

The Mimbres phase in the Upper Gila is represented by very large stone masonry pueblos with black-on-white and indented corrugated pottery, small square "kivas" and large rectangular masonry great kivas (Lekson 1990). Mimbres burials were typically subfloor inhumations, accompanied by a single bowl inverted over the head. Almost always, ceramic vessels in burials were "killed," that is, a small hole (1–2 cm in diameter) was punched out of the bottom of the vessel. Other ancient societies killed mortuary vessels, but this practice was particularly characteristic during the Man-

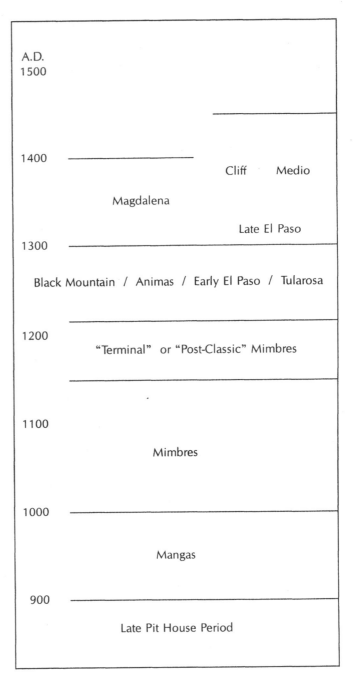

Figure 1.2. Chronology of southwestern New Mexico.

gas and Mimbres phases, and vessels with "kill holes" were recovered from the Dutch Ruin. The Mangas and Mimbres phases represent the highest population levels in the Upper Gila (Lekson 1990a, 1992c). It appears likely that agriculture was based on canal irrigation (Lekson 1986). The Mimbres phase ended between A.D. 1130 and 1150, and thereafter there is only limited evidence of occupation of the Upper Gila until the late thirteenth-or fourteenth-century Salado.

For this late interval, the Salado of the Upper Gila is termed the Cliff phase (Nelson and LeBlanc 1986); it is characterized by large adobe pueblos with Gila and Tonto polychrome pottery. Kivas apparently were not built at most of these Salado settlements, although presumably certain rooms were used for ceremonial purposes (Wallace 1998). Whereas earlier Mimbres phase walls were full height with roughly coursed stone masonry, the later Cliff phase walls were usually (but not always) of puddle or coursed adobe, often with a basal reinforcement of rows of upright stones or "cimientos." After the adobe erodes, cimientos often remain as visible rows of cobbles poking up through the crusty desert ground surface. (Archaeologists have identified cimientos at all the sites described below.) It is almost certain that Salado villages in the Upper Gila were dependent on canal irrigation. Salado burial practices in the Upper Gila were remarkably varied and included urn cremation cemeteries, subfloor inhumations, and subfloor urn cremations. Contemporary with the fourteenth-century Salado were the famous city of Paquime (or Casas Grandes) in northern Chihuahua (Di Peso 1974; Schaafsma and Riley 1999; Woosely and Ravesloot 1993) and a less well-known cluster of apparently post-Mesa Verde phase (A.D. 1300–1400?) towns in southwestern Socorro County, New Mexico (Lekson 1996a).

Between the Mimbres phase, which ends about A.D. 1150, and the Cliff or Salado phase, which begins about 1300, there is scant archaeological evidence of settlement in the Upper Gila. Two phases have been proposed, in the past, to fill that gap: Tularosa and Animas. There are several large Tularosa phase sites, marked by Tularosa Black-on-white pottery and dating to the thirteenth century, just to the north and west of the Upper Gila (Brown 1973; Lekson 1996a). The Gila Cliff Dwellings, near the head of the Upper Gila, date to the Tularosa phase and large sites with Tularosa pottery are known from the Safford Valley (Lekson 1996a), but only a thin Tularosa phase presence is evident in the Cliff Valley of the Upper Gila, and it is apparently absent entirely from the Redrock Valley. The Animas phase (Chapter 3) is a taxon with a wonderfully muddled history (Hegmon and others 1999; LeBlanc and Nelson 1976; Lekson 1992a, 1992b). The original definition of the Animas phase was as a locally derived intermediate phase between Mimbres and Salado, and it was once used in that sense in the Upper Gila (Lekson and Klinger 1973). However, the Animas phase, thus employed, has not survived close scrutiny in the Upper Gila (Lekson 1992b).

Following the Mimbres phase, there may have been a gap or hiatus of up to 150 years in the Upper Gila region before the appearance of Salado settlements. The dating of those settlements is a primary concern in this report. By traditional definition, Salado occupation began no earlier than A.D. 1250 and much more likely 1300, and it ended in the Upper Gila perhaps as late as the sixteenth century. Salado constitutes the principal archaeology of the Upper Gila after the Mimbres phase: huge, spectacular, famous sites that are, alas, poorly described or unreported. This curious situation arose in large part because of a privately owned, publicly accessible ruin, Kwilleylekia. This large, late Salado pueblo was operated as an archaeological park by an exceptional avocational archaeologist, Richard "Red" Ellison and his wife Virginia Ellison of Silver City, New Mexico. For many years, the Ellisons excavated the site and charged visitors a small admission to watch the dig, tour the site, and view a small display of artifacts housed in an on-site museum. Kwilleylekia was listed in tourist literature and shown on maps distributed by the American Automobile Association. Other than the Gila Cliff Dwellings National Monument (difficult of access until its long mountain road was paved), Kwilleylekia was for many years the only archaeological site developed for public viewing in southwestern New Mexico and southeastern Arizona.

The 1965 excavation of the large Ormand Ruin as part of a highway salvage program was very public (right on the highway), and it cemented the Cliff Valley's reputation as a major Salado district (Dittert 1966). That reputation was deserved; A. V. Kidder had excavated at a Salado ruin on Duck Creek, and Jack and Vera Mills (1972), another highly respected avocational archaeological couple, excavated a sizable portion of the Salado Dinwiddie site on Duck Creek. Unfortunately, analyses and reports from all these excavations were minimal: Ormand and Dinwiddie were described in brief preliminary reports, and Kwilleylekia was never formally reported.

Cliff Valley Salado sites were sufficiently well known that participants in the 1967 Salado Red Ware Conference declared the Cliff Valley of the Upper Gila an area of Salado colonization (Lindsay and Jennings 1968), which consisted of Plateau or Mogollon Highland peoples intruding into the Upper Gila, (the second model listed above). The Upper Gila Project, a "New Archaeology" enterprise of the early 1970s, recast Cliff Valley Salado as a local development, arguing for continuity from Mimbres to Salado through the Animas phase at sites such as Villareal II (the third model above; Lekson and Klinger 1973). The Mimbres Foundation, also following "New" paradigms, argued for both continuities and discontinuities between Mimbres and Salado, via the Black Mountain phase (a local version of the Animas phase; Nelson and LeBlanc 1986: 247):

> We cannot accept without qualification that population displacement occurred. At the same time we feel, however intuitively, that the changes between Classic Mimbres and Black Mountain periods are indicative of profound reorganization and cultural replacement, if not replacement of the population. Both the temporal rhythm and the stylistic content of these changes point to Casas Grandes, and not to the Salado phenomenon as traditionally conceived.

That is, local populations changed costumes and material cultures (the first model above). Casas Grandes, referred to hereafter as Paquime, attracted post-Mimbres Black Mountain and Animas populations, and the Salado of the Upper Gila represented those populations returning to the north after the fall of Paquime (Nelson and LeBlanc 1986: 245–247).

After this intriguing reconstruction was published, the redating of Paquime to no earlier than A.D. 1250 (Dean and Ravesloot 1993) negated their model of "alternating centrifugal and centripetal [post-Mimbres] population movements centered on Casas Grandes" (Nelson and LeBlanc 1986: 247). The city of Paquime did not exist until 100 or 150 years after the conventional end of Mimbres at 1150.

More recent analyses recognize this new chronology, but maintain the fundamentally local nature of Upper Gila Salado by arguing for migrations within and among the valleys of southwestern New Mexico, culminating in the Cliff phase. Overpopulation of the Cliff Valley resulted in small "spin-off" communities appearing in the then-empty Mimbres Valley (the fourth model above; Nelson and Anyon 1996).

A recent multiauthored summary of "time-space systematics in the post A.D. 1100 Mimbres region" (Hegmon and others 1999) is curiously silent on Salado, the most spectacular post-A.D. 1100 archaeology in the old Mimbres region, ending a brief paragraph with the discouraging conclusion that "the question of continuity between the Black Mountain and Cliff phases remains unresolved and is a good topic for future research" (Hegmon and others 1999: 161).

A recently published analysis of the Ormand Ruin concluded that the Cliff Valley Salado represented a migration into the Upper Gila from "areas of east-central and southeastern Arizona" (Wallace 1998: 409), a return to the second model. Thus we come full circle in the interpretation of Upper Gila Salado, from migrations, to evolutions, and back to migrations. It is time to look at the sites and the information we can glean from them.

SALADO SITES OF THE UPPER GILA

Before introducing Dutch Ruin and Villareal II, it is helpful to present the large Salado sites of the Upper Gila (Figs. 1.1, 1.3). Small Salado sites (a rare breed) are discussed in Chapters 3 and 4, and included in Chapter 4 are considerations of Salado settlement patterns.

Kwilleylekia Ruins

Probably the most famous Salado site in the Cliff Valley of the Upper Gila area is site LA 4935, the Kwilleylekia Ruins (Figs. 1.1, 1.3). Excavated from the 1960s to the 1980s by Richard and Virginia Ellison, Kwilleylekia had more than 200 rooms in two major multistoried adobe room blocks. It produced two cutting tree-ring dates of A.D. 1380, several archaeomagnetic dates, and a remarkable assemblage of whole pots and artifacts, now dispersed without formal study. Kwilleylekia was probably one of the latest and perhaps the last late Salado settlement occupied in the Upper Gila. It appears to have been a single component site. Richard Ellison told me in 1972 that sixteenth-century ceramics were included in the collections, but this statement cannot now be evaluated.

Ormand Ruin

Larry Hammack excavated the Ormand Site (LA 5793; Figs. 1.1, 1.3) in the Cliff Valley in 1965 (Dittert 1966), and a report was prepared by Laurel Wallace (1998). The site consisted of at least 150 rooms in four single-story adobe room blocks around a central plaza. A "ceremonial room" was excavated in the middle of the plaza, and two discrete urn-cremation cemeteries were located at the margins of the pueblo. Earlier Pit House period and Archaic period structures were found under the Salado component. The collections are housed at the Museum of New Mexico in Santa Fe.

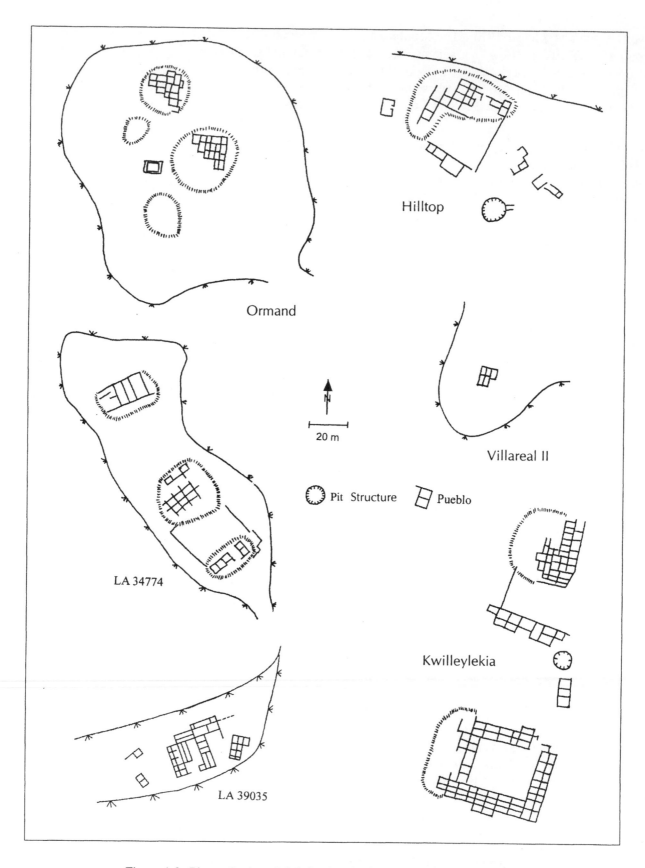

Ormand

Hilltop

LA 34774

Villareal II

⊙ Pit Structure   ⊟ Pueblo

Kwilleylekia

LA 39035

Figure 1.3. Plans of selected Salado sites in the Upper Gila River valley.

Site LA 34774

Site LA 34774 (Fig. 1.3) on Duck Creek had at least 90 rooms in three stone masonry and adobe room blocks, two of which were connected by a compound wall. The mound height was between 2.5 m and 3 m, indicating at least two stories (Chapman and others 1985, Appendix 1: 8). The site had a Mimbres phase component.

Hilltop Ruin

My tentative identification of a site first excavated by Kidder (1962[1924]: 294–296) and later by Hattie and Burton Cosgrove (1929, 1932) is the Hilltop Ruin (Fig. 1.3). Two tree-ring samples were obtained, which produced cutting dates of A.D. 1243. A site mapped by Chapman, Gossett, and Gossett (1985, Appendix 1: 121) is probably Hilltop Ruin. It consisted of 50 rooms in a massive L-shaped stone masonry and adobe room block with a low compound wall enclosing a small plaza. The mound height was 2 m, indicating at least two stories. The site had an earlier Mimbres phase component. Collections may exist at the Peabody Museum, Harvard University, Cambridge.

Site LA 39035

Site LA 39035 (Fig. 1.3) in the Redrock Valley was a stone masonry and adobe complex of about 30 rooms in one large rectangular room block with several detached or isolated rooms or small room blocks. Mimbres and Salado ceramics were recovered in 1977 when I surveyed and mapped the site (Lekson 1978a).

Dinwiddie Site

A site designated as NM S:14:1 (ASM) located on Duck Creek is a large Salado site that should not be confused with the small Mangas phase Dinwiddie Site in the Cliff Valley (Lekson 1999a). Dinwiddie may be the "Pottsville" site of Cosgrove and Cosgrove (1929, 1932). The Salado Dinwiddie settlement was notably large, with more than 100 rooms in two adobe room blocks. The site was partially excavated by Jack and Vera Mills (1972). It produced a large whole vessel collection and two fourteenth-century archaeomagnetic dates, which were curated at Eastern Arizona Community College in Thatcher, Arizona.

Willow Creek Site

The Willow Creek Site, located on a tributary of Mangas Creek, consisted of about 80 rooms in two adobe room blocks. Three rooms were excavated by James E. Fitting (1973). The site had a poorly defined Mimbres component. Following recent vandalism, Gila National Forest personnel completed additional mitigation work.

TJ Ruin

Site LA 54955, the TJ Ruin (Fig. 1.1), is situated above the Upper Box in the "Three Forks" area of the Upper Gila. It is a large Mimbres site with smaller "Animas" or Salado components that probably consisted of two small room blocks (labeled "4" and "5" in McKenna and Bradford 1989, Fig. 4).

Solomonsville Ruin

Also known as Buena Vista, Curtis Ranch, or Pueblo Viejo, the Solomonsville Ruin is in the Safford Valley of the Gila River and outside the Upper Gila as defined herein. However, reference is made to this large and important site and to collections recovered by the University of Colorado in 1931 (Tyberg 2000) and by Jack and Vera Mills (1978). Tyberg (2000: 27) reported that the settlement consisted of:

> a large pueblo compound including evidence of an "older village" and what may be a Hohokam-style "great house," the relatively unexplored remains of an earlier pit-house village, at least one ball court and/or possibly a reservoir, at least one cremation area (and/or several pottery kiln areas), and a proposed canal system.

Dutch Ruin

Dutch Ruin (LA 8706; Fig. 1.4), one of the very largest Salado sites in the Upper Gila, is located near Redrock in Grant County, New Mexico. The settlement had about 150 rooms. Approximately 15 rooms were excavated in the 1960s by avocational archaeologists, who assembled a major whole-vessel ceramic collection and smaller collections of nonceramic artifacts (Chapter 2). The site had a Mimbres phase component.

Figure 1.4. Dutch Ruin, looking northeast.

Figure 1.5. Villareal II, looking east.

Villareal II

Villareal II (Figs. 1.3, 1.5), one of the smallest Salado structural sites in the Upper Gila, is located a few kilometers above the small town of Gila, Grant County, New Mexico. Unlike the sites described above, the settlement at Villareal II had only five rooms. It was excavated by Timothy Klinger and me in 1972 and 1973 and generated a modest collection of sherds, flakes, and other artifacts (Chapter 3, Appendix B).

DUTCH RUIN AND VILLAREAL II

Dutch Ruin and Villareal II constitute two poles of Salado settlement in the Upper Gila; Dutch Ruin is huge, Villareal II is tiny. Together with the sites listed above, and other contextual data, they provide a useful foundation for understanding Salado archaeology of the Upper Gila. But the basis for understanding differs markedly for the two sites: the Dutch Ruin collection is an unsystematic but spectacular whole-vessel assemblage and Villareal II is a carefully excavated, screened sample of potsherds and flakes. I describe these two sites and their collections (Dutch Ruin in Chapter 2; Villareal II in Chapter 3) and use the salvaged information to investigate Salado settlement patterns and discuss the ceramic assemblages at these and other sites (Chapter 4). As case studies, Dutch Ruin and Villareal II represent the range of Upper Gila Salado. More broadly, the sites address the meaning of archaeological continuity and discontinuity. And they demonstrate, I hope, the utility and necessity of rehabilitating old, scorned collections.

The nature of these collections and the nature of Salado require a particular emphasis on ceramics, much more so than might be the case with other Southwestern phenomena, such as the "Chaco phenomenon" in which ceramics play only a minor role. This monograph focuses on pottery, but does not ignore architecture, settlement pattern, and other archaeological data.

Dutch Ruin and Villareal II are both, by contemporary standards, flawed collections. Neither of these sites were excavated as they would be today. Dutch Ruin was the hobby of two inspired amateurs, entranced (by their own accounts) by "sherditis." They had interest and even passion for the work, but only rudimentary notions of context and recording. Villareal II was systematically excavated by a university research project, using standard archaeological techniques of that time, and then left largely unexamined for almost three decades, old data awaiting new questions. Although we know a great deal more about Villareal II than Dutch Ruin, it cannot be denied that the Villareal II data have "decayed" over the last 27 years. Details (and kodachromes) that were clear and crisp in the 1970s are less precise today. In part, this report represents a penitential effort to rehabilitate older collections to address questions of current interest.

The Dutch Ruin and Villareal II collections include a wide variety of stone tools, bone and stone ornaments, and other artifacts. This study, however, emphasizes ceramics. Villareal II was the only Upper Gila Salado site to be systematically screened; thus comparative analyses of chipped stone, fauna, and even sherd assemblage composition are difficult or impossible. These classes of artifacts are briefly described and used in intrasite discussions, but no attempt is made to expand the analyses to regional scales. Ceramics, on the other hand, can be compared across a wide range of sites on at least the whole vessel, typological levels, levels appropriate to some aspects of Salado that are based on decorated painted ceramics.

In presenting the ceramic and architectural data from Dutch Ruin (a large and complex town) and Villareal II (a small farmstead), I address a range of ideas and models previously proposed for the Upper Gila Salado and generate new ideas about the place of Upper Gila Salado in southwestern history. The use of older, unreported collections entails a small number of descriptive passages that are tangential to the principal theme, but these two sites prove to be particularly useful for current questions about the nature and history of Salado.

CHAPTER TWO

Dutch Ruin

Dutch Ruin (LA 8706, NM Y:5:1 ASM) is a large Salado pueblo near Redrock, New Mexico (Fig. 1.1). The site was partially excavated by Ms. Gladys "Grandma" Bennett, an avocational archaeologist from Pinos Altos, New Mexico, and Ms. Nanabell "Dutch" Fortenberry (the property owner) during the mid–1960s, probably from 1963 to May 1968. It has also been called the Fortenberry Site (Nelson and LeBlanc 1986).

Bennett and Fortenberry corresponded with Alexander Lindsay, Jr. (among many other archaeologists), and Lindsay arranged for sherd collections from Dutch Ruin to be placed at the Museum of Northern Arizona, the Arizona State Museum, and the Amerind Foundation. Fortenberry and Bennett (1968) wrote a brief report, copies of which are on file at the Museum of Northern Arizona and the Arizona State Museum. Lindsay alerted other archaeologists to the importance of Dutch Ruin and the existence of a large collection of whole vessels and other artifacts from the site.

Important additional information was contained in a series of photographs of pots and artifacts taken by Fortenberry and Bennett. Some of these photos were included with the brief report (Fortenberry and Bennett 1968) and other loose photos were acquired by LaVerne Herrington, copies of which were supplied to me by Darrell Creel of the Texas Archaeological Research Laboratory.

The majority of the whole and partial ceramic vessels (see Table 2.3), a range of shell, stone, and bone artifacts, and notes from Dutch Ruin were acquired as a collection by the Johnson-Humrickhouse Museum in Coshocton, Ohio, in 1974. A donor had purchased the collection in the late 1960s or early 1970s in New Mexico and then donated it to the museum. Lindsay tracked the collection to Ohio, and I examined and photographed the artifacts in 1998. Copies of photographs and records are now on file at the Arizona State Museum in Tucson and the Laboratory of Anthropology in Santa Fe. (The vast majority of sherds from Dutch Ruin were reportedly reburied at the site.)

In 1974, coincidentally with the arrival of the Dutch Ruin pots at Coshocton, the site itself was mapped and recorded during a survey of the Cliff Valley directed by Roger Moore and me (Lekson 1978a). We made extensive systematic surface collections. Ceramics were analyzed by Charles M. Mobley, with assistance from Emil Haury and Stewart Peckham (Lekson 1978a). The lithic collections were analyzed by Roger Moore. Collections from the 1974 survey are curated at the Laboratory of Anthropology, Museum of Indian Art and Culture, Santa Fe.

The Dutch Ruin is located on a low sandy ridge, apparently a terrace remnant, a few meters above the Gila River floodplain (see Fig. 1.4). The ruin extends for at least 50 m by 100 m under several ranch buildings (reputed to have been a CCC camp headquarters) and over most of the low ridge. An unknown but significant portion of the ruin was used for levees and ditch-building by the landowner previous to Ms. Fortenberry.

The settlement had at least two components comprised of a large Salado pueblo and earlier Mimbres architectural features exposed in several areas beneath the Salado pueblo. In addition, Late Pit House period sherds were found in later contexts, suggesting a third, earlier occupation of the low ridge. There is almost no information on the Mimbres settlement beyond the notation that several vessels were found together "on a Mimbres floor."

The Salado pueblo consisted of massed adobe rooms, of uncertain ground plan. Sketch maps from Fortenberry and Bennett (1968) indicate a ruin of at least 50 rooms. The 1974 field survey estimated 200 rooms, but the site was badly disturbed and individual walls were not evident on the surface. It is safe to suggest that Dutch Ruin was about 150 rooms in size and perhaps significantly larger.

At least fifteen rooms were excavated in a block six rooms long and four rooms wide (Fig. 2.1). The fill of at least one room (Room 4) was described as "yellow sifted sand or clay," which may represent eolian deposi-

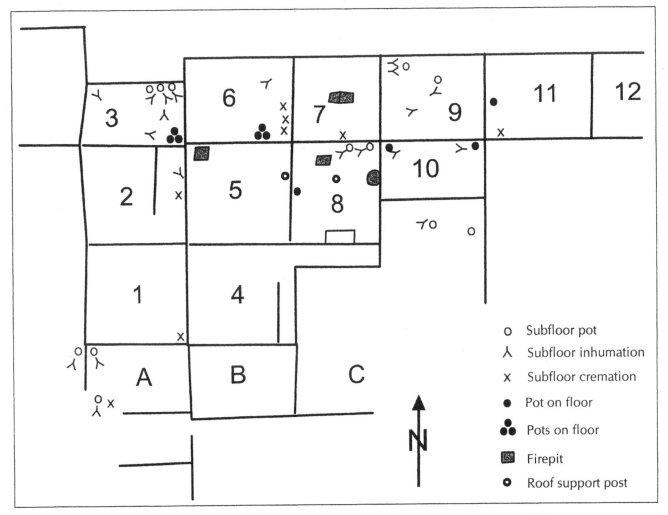

Figure 2.1. Plan of Dutch Ruin excavations (after Fortenberry and Bennett 1968).

tion. Rooms 5, 7, and 8 had rectangular floor features that appear to have been firepits. Room 8 also had a feature described as a "step" at the middle of the south wall, possibly a round firepit on the east wall, and a post at the center of the floor. Room 5 had a post along its east wall. Rooms 3, 6, 8, and 11 had one or more vessels on their floors, including one group of seven vessels (see Table 2.6, Context A), probably from either Room 3 or Room 6. Rooms A, B, and C were each noted as "doesn't seem to have a floor."

Most rooms (9 of 15) contained at least one subfloor inhumation or subfloor cremation or both (Fig. 2.1). Room 10 was noted as having "ten or more" burials, not mapped on the sketch map or shown in Figure 2.1. Several and perhaps all of the cremations were in vessels ("urns"), some of which had inverted bowls as "cover vessels." At least one, and probably several, of the inhumations had vessels inverted over their heads.

As discussed in Chapter 1, many Upper Gila Salado pueblos were built with *cimientos* or upright cobble "footing stones" at the base of the puddled adobe walls. Unfortunately, there is no evidence (positive or negative) for cimientos at Dutch Ruin. No mention was made in the brief report (Fortenberry and Bennett 1968) and no photographs survive that show walls. The field survey of 1974 did not observe preserved cimientos, but the site was so badly disturbed that this negative evidence may be false. In summary, while there is no direct evidence of cimientos, the circumstances of the site's documentation are such that it remains possible that cimientos were present.

Two midden areas were mentioned by Fortenberry and Bennett, but neither was evident in 1974; there was no mention of burials in middens or in cemeteries. "There was no evidence of violence or annihilation at the site, rooms [were] not burned and all skeleton remains [were] buried or cremated" (Fortenberry and Bennett 1968). These sparse sentences are all we know about the site's architecture and stratigraphy. Before turning to the focus of this analysis, the pottery, I record the few observations it was possible to make on the stone and shell material; no provenience within the site is available for any of the nonceramic artifacts.

LITHICS

Stone artifacts include about 50 miscellaneous hammer stones and undifferentiated cobble tools (not discussed further here), and 3 manos, 3 mortars, 6 small stone bowls, 14 obsidian projectile points, 6 axes, 3 palettelike objects, 2 stone pipes, 3 objects that might be pottery anvils, 1 painted cobble, and 9 serpentine artifacts. The three manos are all rectangular, "brick"-shaped tools of fine-grained volcanic ash material. The mortars are small, shallow depressions on river cobbles or roughly shaped cobble-sized volcanic ash stones. The stone bowls are all small (less than 15 cm in diameter), round, with generally shallow interior depressions, made of fine-grained volcanic ash materials (Fig. 2.2). The obsidian projectile points (Fig. 2.3) include a range of small, side-notched, corner-notched, and stemmed forms that appear to span a considerable period of time (typologically, from Late Pit House period or earlier to Late Pueblo period styles). Axes (Fig. 2.4) and mauls are made of a very fine-grained, dense, presumably volcanic stone (perhaps dacite), and all are three-quarter grooved; one maul is of vesicular basalt.

Figure 2.3. Selected obsidian projectile points. (Scale in cm.)

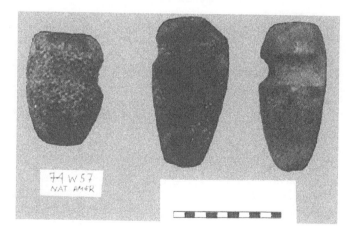

Figure 2.4. Stone axes. (Scale in cm.)

Figure 2.2. Stone artifacts: *top row*, bowl, thick disk, palette?; *bottom row*, bowl, palettes? (Scale in cm.)

Three small palettelike objects (Fig. 2.2) are made of the same material as axes and are small subrectangular slab-shaped objects without obvious grinding surfaces. Two stone pipes (Fig. 2.5) are short, each about 6 cm long and 4 cm wide. The finished piece (Fig. 2.5 *left*) is drilled through and made of rhyolite; the other is unfinished and made of a rhyolitic volcanic ash material. Three mushroom-shaped tools are each about 8 cm tall and 4 cm to 5 cm wide at their widest point; they may be pottery anvils (Fig. 2.6). All three are made of

Figure 2.5. Stone pipes. (Scale in cm.)

Figure 2.7. Painted cobble. (Scale in cm.)

Figure 2.6. Stone anvils, perhaps for manufacturing pottery. (Scale in cm.)

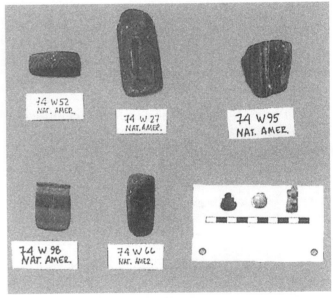

Figure 2.8. Selected serpentine artifacts: *top row*, rod-shaped artifact (left), roughly shaped flat blanks (center, right); *bottom row*, palette fragment? (left), flat blank (center), three carved pendant fragments (right). (Scale in cm.)

a light volcanic ash material. A single painted flat sub-oval cobble, about 16 cm long by 8 cm wide, had faint traces of yellow and dark green-black bands around the outer circumference of its flat upper face (Fig. 2.7).

The nine serpentine (ricolite) artifacts were all worked pieces, a range of small subrectangular forms, effigies, and other shapes (Fig. 2.8). No serpentine debris was present in the Johnson-Humrickhouse collections. Most of the serpentine artifacts were flat, tabular pieces less than 10 cm in maximum dimension; one of them was lightly incised with a chevron pattern. Three effigy or pendant pieces were in the collection. These kinds of artifacts were also found at Paquime, but none of the remarkable Paquime serpentine forms (stools, axe heads, pipes; Di Peso and others 1974a: 188) appeared in the Dutch Ruin collections. Serpentine was a major imported material at Paquime; a total of 114.7 kg was

reported as finished artifacts and unfinished raw material, second only to shell (in weight), and almost a hundred times greater (in weight) than turquoise. Di Peso reported that serpentine at Paquime "came from the Redrock quarries of New Mexico's Grant County, some 282 km north of Paquime. This was discerned by comparative studies of x-ray diffractograms and the presence of phlogopite mica" (Di Peso and others 1974a: 188).

Figure 2.9. Shell and turquoise pendant, restored by the excavators, Nanabell Fortenberry and Gladys Bennett.

SHELL

Shell artifacts include 9 restrung shell or stone and shell bead strands, 18 glycymeris shell bracelets or bracelet fragments, 12 loose shells or shell fragments, and one spectacular composite pendant consisting of a shell covered with turquoise tesserae. Shell species include conus, olivella, turritella, and glycymeris, among others, but these identifications should be considered tentative. Jewelry included at least 200 turquoise beads and pendants.

The majority of shell and turquoise beads had been restrung; it is impossible to evaluate the accuracy or association of the restrung beads. It is likely that beads from various contexts were combined into "necklaces" and "bracelets," so no further descriptions are provided here. One artifact, however, is notable: a bivalve shell with turquoise tesserae and recycled pendants affixed to half of the piece (Fig. 2.9). Field notes indicate that "marks on shell allowed exact replacement of turquoise" and there is no reason to doubt that this artifact, as restored, appears much as it was originally constructed.

CERAMICS

Table 2.1 lists the decorated sherd percentages from collections obtained in 1974, with additional types reported by Fortenberry and Bennett but not represented in the 1974 surface collection. Fortenberry and Bennett (1968) included a long list of types represented by vessels at the Dutch Ruin that they compiled with the assistance of a remarkable list of distinguished archaeologists who apparently examined sherds from the site. Some of the types represented in Table 2.1 (more than 35) could, of course, reflect multiple different identifications of the same or similar sherds by different archaeologists, but even so comparison with other Upper Gila sites suggests that the Salado assemblage at Dutch Ruin is in fact remarkably diverse. The list clearly reflects the two components present, with about ten decorated types representing the earlier Mimbres occupation. Although this study focuses on the Salado assemblage, two observations made about the Mimbres ceramics by Fortenberry and Bennett are worth repeating here. First, they note that sherds of Mimbres Style II (which they called "Oak Canyon Black-on-white") were much more numerous than sherds of later Mimbres Classic Style III. They suggest that higher proportions of Style II and lower proportions of Style III "may mean the Mimbres people left this site [Dutch Ruin] and maybe the entire area [Redrock Valley] before abandoning their homes on the Mimbres River." This conclusion, while intriguing, is not borne out by survey data (Lekson 1978a, 1992b). Second, they note a "remarkable" proportion of flare-rim bowl forms among the Mimbres series black-on-white sherds. (Flare-rimmed Mimbres vessels in the Upper Gila are generally Style III.)

Table 2.2 provides the percentages of plain, corrugated, and textured sherds in the 1974 survey sample. Charles M. Mobley (with the assistance of several archaeologists) classified the plain, corrugated, and textured ceramics reported from the Dutch Ruin (see Table 2.4). Because we used a descriptive typology in 1974 rather than the Southwestern binomial typology used by Fortenberry and Bennett, the two analyses of these sherds are not integrated into a single list.

A list of whole or partial vessels from the Dutch Ruin is in Table 2.3. Of the 83 listed items, 72 vessels were observed in the Johnson-Humrickhouse Museum collections. I use the vessel number for identification herein and the corresponding figure number is in Table 2.3. The vessel numbers represent the last digit or digits of the Johnson-Humrickhouse Museum catalogue numbers. Ten additional vessels, not present in the Johnson-Humrickhouse collections, appeared individually or in groups of pots in photographs taken during the excavations by Fortenberry and Bennett (1968, and loose photographs provided by Darrell Creel). Although not illustrated here, they are identified as X–1 through X–10 in

Table 2.1. Painted and Decorated Ceramic Types Reported from the Dutch Ruin

Ceramics	% in 1974 collections N = 468 (Lekson 1978a)	Reported by Fortenberry and Bennett (1968)
Mogollon Red-on-brown		*
Three Circle Red-on-white		*
Mimbres Style I-II Black-on-white	0.6	
Mimbres Style III Black-on-white	1.9	
Mimbres Polychrome		*
Mimbres Black-on-white undif.	2.3	
Mimbres White Ware	0.2	
Kiatuthlanna Black-on-white		*
Red Mesa Black-on-white		*
Reserve Black-on-white	0.2	
Tularosa Black-on-white	1.5	
Undif. Zuni Black-on-white	0.2	
Chupadero Black-on-white	6.0	
Three Rivers Red-on-terracotta		*
El Paso Polychrome	8.5	
Tucson Polychrome	6.4	
Maverick Mountain Polychrome		*
Pinto Polychrome		*
Tonto Polychrome	2.6	
Gila Polychrome	63.0	
Wingate Black-on-red	1.5	
St. Johns Polychrome	1.7	
Nantack Polychrome		*
Fourmile Polychrome		*
Cibicue Polychrome		*
Heshotauthla Polychrome		*
Querino Polychrome		*
Rio Grande Glaze "D or E"[?]		*
Babicora Polychrome		*
Carretas Polychrome		*
Dublan Polychrome		*
Huerigos Polychrome		*
Villa Ahumada Polychrome		*
Ramos Polychrome	1.0	
Chihuahua undif.	1.0	
Unidentified black-on-white	0.4	
Unidentified red-on-white	0.2	
Unidentified red-on-brown	0.8	
Encinas Red-on-brown		*
San Carlos Red-on-brown		*
Sacaton Red-on-buff		*

NOTE: Additionally Stephen Lekson observed a mug of either Mesa Verde Black-on-white or Magdalena Black-on-white in 1998 in the Johnson-Humrickhouse collections; neither type was represented in the 1974 collections nor listed by Fortenberry and Bennett (1968).

Table 2.2. Plain, Corrugated, and Textured Ceramics Reported from the Dutch Ruin Surface Collections in 1974

Ceramics (N = 1,981)	%
Plain, polished exterior,	
plain interior	2.0
polished smudged interior	0.5
unpolished smudged interior	0.5
Plain, unpolished exterior,	
plain interior	48.0
polished smudged interior	1.0
unpolished smudged interior	22.5
Corrugated, plain interior,	1.0
polished smudged interior	0.5
unpolished smudged interior	1.0
Indented corrugated,	
plain interior	1.0
unpolished smudged interior	2.0
Incised, plain interior	4.0
Incised, unpolished, smudged interior	0.5
Tooled/indented,	
polished exterior, unpolished smudged interior	0.5
unpolished exterior, plain interior	3.0
unpolished exterior, polished smudged interior	0.5
unpolished exterior, unpolished smudged interior	0.5
Cord-marked	1.0
Red-slipped exterior,	
plain interior	2.0
red-slipped interior	8.0

From Lekson 1978a

Table 2.3. Of the 74 Johnson-Humrickhouse catalogue numbers, vessel 65 was not from Dutch Ruin and is not included here. Vessel 20, a St. Johns Polychrome bowl, had been deaccessioned; it almost certainly was represented in a photograph and is numbered here X–5. Vessel 70 was listed in the museum catalogue but not available for observation while I was there; it is excluded from this analysis. Thus the inventory considered here equals 81 whole or partial vessels.

Overlap between museum records, notes, and photographs make it reasonably certain that these vessels came from the Dutch Ruin, but it is possible that a few vessels from other sites were added to the Dutch Ruin collections. (Three historic pueblo pieces catalogued in this accession series were obviously not from Dutch Ruin, but they were clearly marked in the museum records as "not from Dutch Ruin.") In particular, a Mesa Verde or Magdalena Black-on-white mug (Vessel 68) is troublesome. It does not appear in any of the photos of vessels from the Dutch Ruin, nor is Mesa Verde Black-on-white included among the lists of types represented (Fortenberry and Bennett 1968). However, several other

Table 2.3. Dutch Ruin Whole Vessels

Fig. No.	Vessel No.	Height (inches)	Description	Fig. No.	Vessel No.	Height (inches)	Description
2.15a	1	2.5	Gila Polychrome "submarine" vessel, two holes in rim	2.13e	35	4.0	Red slipped jar ("found with Mimbres") ["Salado Red"]
2.15b	2	3.2	Gila Polychrome bowl	2.13f	36	4.5	Red-slipped corrugated jar
2.15c	3	2.75	Gila Polychrome bowl	2.13g	37	10.5	Red-slipped Incised (Playas?) jar
2.16a	4	4.5	Gila Polychrome bowl, with kill hole	2.17e	38	4.5	Tucson Polychrome bowl, with kill hole
2.12	5	4.0	Smudged polished interior, corrugated exterior bowl	2.16h	39	3.5	Gila Polychrome bowl, with kill hole
2.19f	6	4.5	Chupadero Black-on-white pitcher	2.10c	40	3.0	Plain brown bowl
2.17a	7	5.0	Tucson Polychrome bowl, with kill hole	2.16i	41	3.0	Gila Polychrome bowl, with kill hole
2.16b	8	5.0	Gila Polychrome jar	2.16j	42	6.0	Gila Polychrome bowl (no kill hole)
2.18d	9	8.0	Ramos Polychrome jar	2.19d	43	4.5	El Paso Polychrome jar
2.18a, b	10	6.0	Ramos Polychrome effigy jar, man smoking pipe	2.16m	44	3.0	Tonto Polychrome bowl, with kill hole
2.13a	11	4.0	Red-slipped (Cloverdale?) Corrugated jar	2.10g	45	5.0	Plain brown (Alma Plain ?) jar, "found on floor of room"
2.10h	12	5.0	Plain Brown (Alma Plain?) jar	2.23c	46		Mimbres Style II Black-on-white scoop
2.16c	13	4.0	Gila Polychrome jar ("seed jar")	2.10i	47	3.5	Polished brown jar
2.23a	14	4.5	Mimbres Style III Black-on-white bowl ["cover bowl over bead jar"]	2.17d	48	3.5	Tucson Polychrome bowl
2.13b	15	3.75	Red-slipped Tooled (Playas?) bowl, with kill hole	2.16k	49	5.5	Gila Polychrome bowl, with kill hole(?)
2.19g	16	5.0	Chupadero Black-on-white pitcher	2.16l	50	3.75	Gila Polychrome bowl, with kill hole
2.10f	17	2.5	Alma Scored(?) bowl	2.13h	51	1.75	Red-slipped bowl, contained gastropods, stones
2.19a	18	7.75	El Paso Polychrome jar	2.19e	52	2.5	El Paso Polychrome bowl
2.15d	19	2.5	Gila Polychrome bowl	2.19i	53	4.2	Chupadero Black-on-white pitcher
	20		St. Johns Polychrome bowl, see X–5	2.13i	54	12.0	Red-slipped (Cloverdale?) Corrugated jar, "found on floor of room"
2.19h	21	8.25	Chupadero Black-on-white pitcher	2.17f	55	4.6	Tucson or Maverick Mountain(?) Polychrome bowl (badly eroded; white outlining has vanished; white flecks in photo are modern storage materials)
2.13d	22	8.25	Red-slipped Tooled (Playas?) jar (cremation urn)				
2.13c	23	2.5	Red-slipped (Playas?) jar	2.18c	56	9.25	Ramos Polychrome(?) effigy jar (badly restored and repainted)
2.17b	24	5.0	Tucson Polychrome bowl, cover bowl for cremation	2.18f	57	4.5	Villa Ahumada Polychrome jar
2.19b	25	5.0	El Paso Polychrome jar (cremation urn)	2.11	58	14.25	Indented corrugated jar
2.16d	26	4.3	Gila Polychrome jar	2.20	59	5.5	Wingate Black-on-red(?) bowl, with kill hole
2.16e	27	3.5	Gila Polychrome bowl, with kill hole	2.10e	60	8.0	Plain brown jar
2.23b	28	1.8	Mimbres Style II-III Black-on-white bowl, miniature	2.16n	61	4.5	Gila Polychrome bowl, with kill hole
2.10b	29	2.0	Plain brown bowl, with kill hole(?)	2.14a	62	4.75	Playas Red bowl
2.16f	30	4.0	Gila Polychrome bowl, with kill hole	2.14b	63	5.5	Red-slipped (Cloverdale?) Corrugated jar
2.17c	31	4.5	Tucson Polychrome bowl, with kill hole	2.14c	64	5.5	Playas(?) Red-slipped jar
2.19c	32	4.5	El Paso Polychrome bowl, with kill hole	2.14d	66	3.75	Red-slipped Cord-impressed (Playas?) jar
2.10d	33	4.0	Plain brown seed jar with suspension lugs, (contained otolith beads)	2.22a	67	4.2	Red Mesa Black-on-white pitcher
2.16g	34	2.5	Gila Polychrome bowl (burned)	2.21	68	2.25	Mesa Verde or Magdalena Black-on-white mug

Table 2.3. Dutch Ruin Whole Vessels *(continued)*

Fig. No.	Vessel No.	Height (inches)	Description	Vessel No.	Height (inches)	Description
2.10a	69	2.5	Plain brown bowl	X–3		Unknown (Gila?) polychrome jar
	70	2.0	Bowl*	X–4		El Paso Polychrome jar
2.18e	71	1.5	Ramos Polychrome bowl	X–5	6.0	St. Johns Polychrome bowl (deaccessioned, 74 B 20)
2.22b	72		Cibola White Ware, black-on-white ladle	X–6		Brown ware effigy jar fragment
2.22c	73		Cibola White Ware, black-on-white scoop	X–7		Gila Polychrome bowl, miniature
2.23d	74		Mimbres Style I Black-on-white scoop	X–8		Gila Polychrome bowl, with kill hole
	X–1		Mimbres Style I Black-on-white bowl fragment	X–9		Gila Polychrome bowl
	X–2		El Paso Polychrome jar	X–10		Tucson Polychrome bowl

NOTES

Vessel No. is the Johnson-Humrickhouse Museum catalogue number; each number is preceeded by the accession prefix "74 B." "X" numbers indicate vessels depicted in the 1968 site photographs that are not currently in the Johnson-Humrickhouse collections.

Heights in inches are approximate, from the Johnson-Humrickhouse Museum catalogue. The scale in the figures herein (the 1998 photographs) is 10 cm.

* Not observed at the Johnson-Humrickhouse Museum and not included in the present analysis.

Table 2.4. Plain, Corrugated, and Textured Ceramic Types Reported from the Dutch Ruin by Fortenberry and Bennett in 1968

Alma Plain	Cloverdale Gouged
Alma Scored	Cloverdale Cord-marked
San Francisco Red	
Mimbres Red-wash	Jornada Brown
	El Paso Brown
Alma Neck Corrugated	
Three Circle Neck Corrugated	Belford Red
Exuberant Corrugated	Belford Brown
McDonald Corrugated	Belford Brown Perforated Rim
McDonald Patterned Corrugated	
Reserve Plain Corrugated	Playas Red Incised
Reserve Indented Corrugated	
Reserve Corrugated Smudged	Ramos Black
Reserve Indented Corrugated Smudged	
Tularosa Fillet-rim	Gila Plain
Salado Fillet-rim	Salt Red

NOTE: Additionally Stephen Lekson observed Cloverdale Corrugated, Playas Red, and Playas Cord-impressed in 1998 in the Johnson-Humrickhouse collections, types not reported by Fortenberry and Bennett (1968).

vessels known to be from Dutch Ruin from notes or other records were also not represented in the surviving photographs. Thus, it is within reason that the Mesa Verde or Magdalena Black-on-white mug came from the Dutch Ruin and its presence is reviewed at the conclusion of this volume.

The types and wares represented by these 81 vessels (Table 2.5) in general agree with the 1974 surface collections (for excellent summary type descriptions, see Nelson and LeBlanc 1986 and Wilson 1998). The whole vessel collection is discussed by the following types and wares: (1) plain brown, (2) indented corrugated, (3) red-

Table 2.5. Frequency of Vessel Forms and Kill Holes by Ceramic Ware and Type

Ware or type	Bowls	Jars and pitchers	Other	"Kill-holes"
Mimbres White Ware	3		2	
Cibola White Ware		1	2	
Chupadero Black-on-white		4		
El Paso Polychrome	2	5		1
Salado polychromes	17	4	1	10
Tucson Polychrome	7			3
Chihuahua polychromes	1	4		
White Mtn. Red Ware	2			1
Mesa Verde or Magdalena Black-on-white			1	
Red slipped	3	10		1
Corrugated		1		
Smudged polished interior	1			
Plain brown ware	4	5	1	1

slipped, (4) smudged polished interior, corrugated exterior bowls, (5) Salado polychrome types, (6) Tucson Polychrome, (7) Chihuahua polychrome types, (8) El Paso Polychrome, (9) Chupadero Black-on-White, (10) White Mountain Red Ware types, (11) Mesa Verde or Magdalena Black-on-white, (12) Cibola White Ware types, and (13) Mimbres White Ware types.

Plain Brown Vessels

Four bowls, four jars, one globular vessel, and one effigy fragment are plain brown pottery. Three of the bowls (Vessels 29, 40, 69; Fig. 2.10*b*, *c*, *a*) are small, shallow simple open forms; the fourth (Vessel 17; Fig. 2.10*f*) is a small, deep, scored bowl with an almost pointed base. All four are smoothed but not polished, and Vessel 17 is lightly scored. When first observed, the form of this vessel suggested a possible Apache affiliation, but it was "found together" with a Mimbres White Ware vessel on a floor (Table 2.6, Context E), and it seems likely to be a variant of Alma Scored. Bowl 29 (Fig. 2.10*b*) has a kill hole. Three of the jars (Vessels 12, 45, 47; Fig. 2.10*h*, *g*, *i*) are small (about 10 cm maximum diameter) with everted rims; the fourth (Vessel 60; Fig. 2.10*e*) is similar in shape and finish but more than twice as large. All four are smoothed or lightly polished. Vessel 33 (Fig. 2.10*d*) is a small globular vessel with two perforated lugs, presumably for suspension. Its orifice is damaged, but apparently was a simple hole about 2 cm in diameter. The vessel is highly polished but apparently not slipped, and it was found in direct association with Gila Polychrome vessels (Table

Table 2.6. Context of Associated Vessels at the Dutch Ruin

Vessel	
	Context A. "Cache," probably on room floor.
1	Gila Polychrome "submarine" vessel
13	Gila Polychrome neckless jar ("seed jar")
19	Gila Polychrome bowl
26	Gila Polychrome jar
36	Red-slipped corrugated jar
53	Chupadero Black-on-white pitcher
X–10	Tucson Polychrome bowl
	Context B. Found together, probably with subfloor inhumation burial (age and sex unknown).
3	Gila Polychrome bowl
4	Gila Polychrome bowl, with kill hole
32	El Paso Polychrome bowl, with kill hole
33	Plain brown seed jar with suspension lugs, contained otolith beads
	Context C. Found together, probably with subfloor inhumation burial (age and sex unknown).
5	Corrugated bowl, with smudged polished interior
15	Playas Red Tooled bowl, with kill hole
	Context D. Found together, with subfloor inhumation burial (probably adult, sex unknown).
2	Gila Polychrome bowl
6	Chupadero Black-on-white pitcher
9	Ramos Polychrome jar
10	Ramos Polychrome effigy jar
27	Gila Polychrome bowl, with kill hole
	Context E. Found together on "Mimbres floor."
17	Alma Scored(?) bowl
28	Mimbres Style II–III Black-on-white bowl, miniature
X–6	Brown ware effigy jar fragment
	Context F. Cremation, probably subfloor.
24	Tucson Polychrome bowl, cover bowl inverted over #25
25	El Paso Polychrome jar, cremation urn
	Context G. Cremation, probably subfloor.
22	Playas Tooled jar, cremation urn
	Context H. "Found on floor of room," probably the same room.
45	Alma Plain (?) jar
54	Cloverdale(?) Corrugated jar
	Context I. Vessel 14 was a "cover bowl over bead jar," another unknown vessel.
14	Mimbres Style III Black-on-white "cover bowl"

Figure 2.10. Vessels of plain brown ware from Dutch Ruin. Table 2.3 Vessel No.: *a*, 69; *b*, 29; *c*, 40; *d*, 33; *e*, 60; *f*, 17; *g*, 45; *h*, 12; *i*, 47. (Scale in cm.)   →

a

b

c

d

e

f

g

h

i

2.6, Context B). It contained an unknown number of otolith beads. (Otoliths are "bones from the inner ears of large fish," identified by Thomas W. Mathews, then of the National Park Service; Fortenberry and Bennett 1968.) Plain brown sherds constituted almost 60 percent of the 1974 surface collections. A problematic textured brown ware effigy fragment (Vessel X–6) was illustrated in an early photograph. From the small portion visible, it apparently was a small jar, possibly a "duck pot," with many tiny indentations on the body and the remnants of a head(?) projecting from the rim.

Indented Corrugated Jar

There is only one nonslipped indented corrugated jar (Vessel 58; Fig. 2.11) in the whole vessel collection. Sherds of indented corrugated were rare (less than 1%) in the 1974 surface collections (compare to Villareal II, Table 3.1). The jar is spherical with a moderately everted rim. There is no patterning to the indentations, which continue up to the edge of the rim.

Figure 2.11. Indented corrugated jar.
Table 2.3 Vessel 58. (Scale in cm.)

Corrugated Exterior Bowl

One bowl with smudged polished interior and corrugated exterior (Vessel 5; Fig. 2.12) has "mending holes" along a crack that developed during its use. It was in a burial with a red-slipped tooled bowl (Vessel 15; Fig. 2.13b; Table 2.6, Context C). This vessel represents a manufacturing technique fairly common on vessels in many thirteenth- and fourteenth-century sites in southern New Mexico. Smudged polished interior bowl sherds constitute about three percent of the total 1974 collection, a frequency greater than that of most decorated and painted types at Dutch Ruin, except Gila Polychrome.

Figure 2.12. Corrugated exterior bowl.
Table 2.3 Vessel 5. (Scale in cm.)

Red-slipped Vessels

A wide range of forms and secondary surface treatments appears in red-slipped polished vessels (Figs. 2.13; 2.14). Several of them are conformable with Playas Red; others could easily be Salado Red or Gila Red. The collection includes a small simple bowl (Vessel 51; Fig. 2.13h); a large simple bowl (Vessel 62; Fig. 2.14a); a large tooled bowl (Vessel 15; Fig. 2.13b); three small jars (Vessels 23, 35, 64; Figs. 2.13c, e; 2.14c); three larger tooled jars (Vessels 22, 37, 66; Figs. 2.13d, g; 2.14d); and four red-slipped corrugated jars (Vessels 11, 36, 54, 63; Figs. 2.13a, f, i; 2.14b). Red-slipped nonpainted sherds constituted more than eight percent of the total 1974 sherd assemblage. The large tooled bowl (Fig. 2.13b) has three rows of closely spaced punctations on the exterior just below the rim; the effect is not unlike

Figure 2.13. Red-slipped vessels. Table 2.3 Vessel No.: *a*, 11; *b*, 15; *c*, 23; *d*, 22; *e*, 35; *f*, 36; *g*, 37; *h*, 51; *i*, 54. (Scale in cm.)

a

b

Figure 2.14. Red-slipped vessels. Table 2.3 Vessel No.: *a*, 62; *b*, 63; *c*, 64; *d*, 66. (Scale in cm.)

c

d

a "fillet" rim (for example, Tularosa Fillet-rim). This vessel has a kill hole and was in a burial in association with Vessel 5 (see Fig. 2.12), a bowl with a smudged polished interior and corrugated exterior. Two of the small red-slipped jars have moderately long, vertical direct rims. Vessel 35 (Fig. 2.13*e*) was reported to have been "found with Mimbres" and (although identified by Fortenberry and Bennett as "Salado Red") it could easily be a late Mimbres red-slipped vessel. Vessel 23 (Fig. 2.13*c*) has a strong sharp angle at the juncture of neck and body. Vessel 64 (Fig. 2.14*c*) is a large spherical jar with a short, moderately everted rim, much like that of the plain ware jars described above. The three tooled Vessels 22, 37, and 66 (Fig. 2.13*d*, *g*; Fig. 2.14*d*) could readily be classified as Playas Red; Vessel 22 (a cremation urn) is textured; Vessel 37 is incised in a banded pattern of hachured triangles; Vessel 66 is cordmarked. Three large red-slipped corrugated jars (Fig.

2.13*f*, *i*; Fig. 2.14*b*) are slipped over unindented corrugations, and the fourth smaller jar (Vessel 11) has a patterned indention reminiscent of Cloverdale Corrugated.

Salado Polychromes

The Salado polychrome types (Figs. 2.15, 2.16), Tonto, Pinto, and Gila, constitute the most frequent painted or decorated types in the whole vessel collection and in the 1974 surface collections, where Salado polychromes equal about 66 percent of the decorated vessels and 13 percent of the total collection. Sixteen subhemispherical bowls (13 illustrated), a miniature bowl (not illustrated), four jars, and one "submarine" shaped pot total 22 vessels. All the whole vessels are typologically Gila Polychrome, except for Vessel X–3 (which may not be a Salado polychrome) and Vessel 44

a

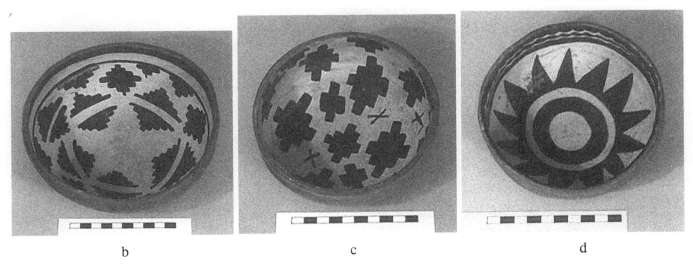

b   c   d

Figure 2.15. Gila Polychrome vessels. Table 2.3 Vessel No.: *a*, 1; *b*, 2; *c*, 3; *d*, 19. (Scale in cm.)

(Fig. 2.16*m*), which is a Tonto Polychrome bowl. Small quantities of Tonto Polychrome were found in the 1974 surface collections, and Fortenberry and Bennett reported the presence of Pinto Polychrome. Terminology for design classes and styles follows Patricia Crown (1994).

Rims on the 16 subhemispherical bowls are either direct or slightly everted (usually with a separate band design on the everted surface); 8 rims are direct and 8 are everted forms. Four design classes are defined in the subhemispherical bowls: banded, offset quartered, repeated elements, and center focused.

Four bowls have framed banded designs and one bowl (Vessel 2; Fig. 2.15*b*) has an unframed banded design

that approaches a "repeated element" pattern. Three of the framed banded bowls (Vessels 34, 49, 50; Fig. 2.16*g*, *k*, *l*) are of Gila style; the fourth (Vessel 19; Fig. 2.15*d*) is of undefined style, a bold pattern that could be interpreted as a center-focused flower design. Of banded bowls, all have direct rims except Vessel 49 (Fig. 2.16*k*), which has an everted rim. Two of the banded bowls appear to have kill holes.

Nine bowls have offset quartered designs, with four (Vessels 27, 30, 41, X–8; Fig. 2.16*e*, *f*, *i*) having a "half-negative" layout; that is, two of the four quarters are negatively offset. One bowl (Vessel X–9) is of uncertain style; two bowls (Vessels 42, X–8; Fig. 2.16*j*) are of Pinedale Stage 4 style; Vessels 4, 27, 30, 39, 41

Figure 2.16. Gila Polychrome vessels (*continued next page*).

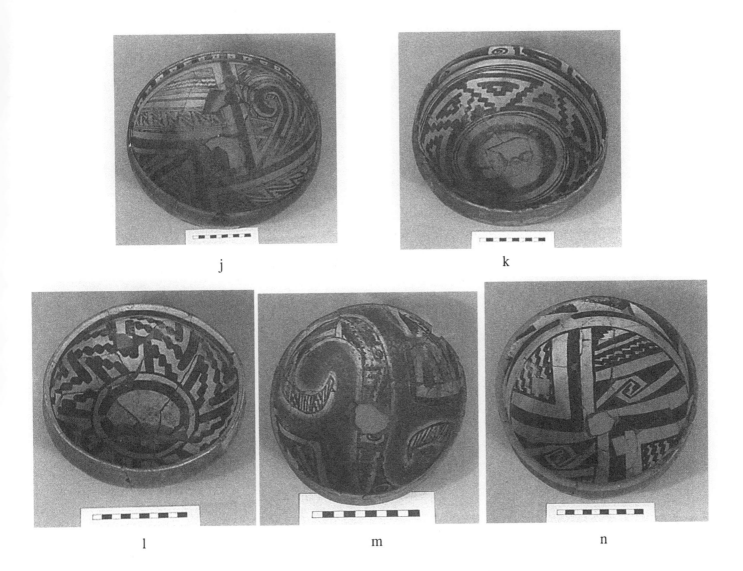

j k

l m n

Figure 2.16. Gila Polychrome vessels and a Tonto Polychrome bowl (*m*). Table 2.3 Vessel No.: *a*, 4; *b*, 8; *c*, 13; *d*, 26; *e*, 27; *f*, 30; *g*, 34; *h*, 39; *i*, 41; *j*, 42; *k*, 49; *l*, 50; *m*, 44; *n*, 61.

(Figs. 2.16*a*, *e*, *f*, *h*, *i*) are of Roosevelt Stage 3 style. Pinedale style bowl Vessel X–8 has a direct rim; Vessel 42 has an everted rim. All but one (Vessel 41) of the Roosevelt style bowls have everted rims. Seven of the offset quartered bowls (Vessels 4, 27, 30, 39, 41, 61, X–8)) have kill holes. One bowl (Vessel 3; Fig. 2.15*c*) has a bold "double terrace" motif as a repeated element (or "wallpaper" pattern). This small bowl has a direct rim and lacks any framing or "life line" below the rim. It does not have a kill hole.

The only Tonto Polychrome bowl (Vessel 44; Fig. 2.16*m*) has a center-focused Escondida style design. This vessel has a direct rim and lacks a broad framing or "life line" on the interior of the rim. It has a kill hole.

Dutch Ruin bowls of the Salado polychromes are smaller than bowls of other decorated types. Patricia Crown (1994) defined three size classes of Salado polychrome bowls (small, medium, and large). Dutch Ruin Gila Polychrome bowls tend to be small, with most diameters less than 12 cm to 15 cm, compared to Crown's "small" average diameter of about 17 cm (Crown 1994, Table 4.9). Indeed, only Vessels 4 and 30 (Fig. 2.16*a*, *f*) can be considered "medium" sized bowls (about 28 cm in diameter), and only Vessels 42 and 49 (Fig. 2.16*j*, *k*) approach the "large" (about 35 cm in diameter) size. This distribution of 12 "small," 2 "medium," and 2 "large" bowls is not unusual for assemblages of the Salado polychromes (Crown 1994, Table 4.9).

Figure 2.17. Tucson Polychrome vessels; *f* is badly eroded and may be Maverick Mountain Polychrome. Table 2.3 Vessel No.: *a*, 7; *b*, 24; *c*, 31; *d*, 48; *e*, 38; *f*, 55. (Scale in cm.)

About two-thirds of the Salado polychrome bowls from Dutch Ruin have everted rims, a form that appears to be particularly frequent in Upper Gila and Chihuahua collections (Lekson 2000). The proportion of everted rims across the entire Salado region is only about 17 percent (Crown 1994, Table 4.5) and most of those vessels are, of course, from Chihuahua or the Upper Gila sites. The proportions of everted rims for Salado assemblages outside the Upper Gila and Chihuahua subregions are not available, but they must be low.

The four Salado polychrome jars are different and distinct in form. Vessels 8, 13, 26 (Fig. 2.16*b*, *c*, *d*) are of Pinedale Stage 4 style; the fourth jar (Vessel X–3) may not even be Gila Polychrome. The three Pinedale-style jars are ovoid in body; that is, their diameter is larger than their height to the neck. Vessel 13 (Fig. 2.16*c*) has no neck or rim and can be considered a "seed jar" or *tecomate*, a rare form in Salado polychromes

according to Patricia Crown (September 7, 2000). Vessel 8 (Fig. 2.16*b*) has a short and slightly everted neck. Vessel 26 (Fig. 2.16*d*) has a slightly taller neck with sufficient rim eversion to support a thin banded design on the rim interior. The fourth jar (Vessel X–3) appears in the early photographs, but it was not present in the Johnson-Humrickhouse collections. It is an unusual form, with the bottom half consisting of a plain, polished, possibly unslipped bowl form, with a slightly everted rim; the upper half is a broad-necked jar with an everted rim and a black-on-white banded design of bold opposed triangles with interlocked frets. The early notes suggest that it is Gila Polychrome, and it is impossible to dismiss this identification based solely on second-generation photographs; however, this vessel may not fit any named type.

Two unusual forms complete the Salado polychrome group: a "submarine" (or "football") shaped pot (Vessel 1; Fig. 2.15a) and a miniature Gila Polychrome bowl (Vessel X–7) with a two-headed bird image in a center-focus design.

Tucson Polychrome Vessels

The type Tucson Polychrome (Fig. 2.17) is represented by six large, deep bowls with the characteristic incurved form and slightly everted rims and by one shallow simple direct-rim bowl (Vessel 55; Fig. 2.17f) that is typologically problematic. All six incurved, everted-rim bowls have exterior band designs and no interior design. Five (Vessels 7, 24, 31, 38, X–10; Fig. 2.17a, b, c, e) have broad black designs without hachure, outlined by thin white lines. Two of these five (Vessels 24 and X–10) also contain single wide white lines as design elements. The sixth incurved bowl (Vessel 38; Fig. 2.17e) has the same design scheme, but has small areas of "squiggle" hachure along the top and bottom of the band. The strong broad-lined designs and the near absence of hachure are characteristic of Tucson Polychrome (Lindsay 1992). Photographs of these vessels were examined by Alexander Lindsay, who noted on 4 October 2000 that they were almost certainly Tucson Polychrome and not the related type Maverick Mountain Polychrome.

The shallow subhemispherical Tucson or Maverick Mountain polychrome bowl (Vessel 55; Fig. 2.17f) has been badly burned. It is painted on the interior only with bold, broad lines outlined with thin white lines; the design is unbanded and perhaps an offset quartered layout. Because of the burning, the white outlines have nearly disappeared. The identification of this bowl as Tucson or Maverick Mountain Polychrome is tenuous, and Lindsay told me (16 September 2000) that he felt it was neither type. Tucson Polychrome bowls are all "large," in Crown's (1994) classification.

Chihuahua Polychromes

Possibly five vessels represent Chihuahua polychrome types (Fig. 2.18), three of Ramos Polychrome, one of Villa Ahumada Polychrome, and one of unknown type. The three Ramos Polychrome vessels include one human effigy jar (Vessel 10; Fig. 2.18a, b), one tall jar with everted rim (Vessel 9; Fig. 2.18d), and one small shallow bowl (Vessel 71; Fig. 2.18e). The human effigy jar represents a man kneeling on one knee, holding a tube to his mouth (smoking a pipe or cane cigarette?). The designs on the sides of the figure include a macaw motif. The tall jar is a classic Ramos Polychrome vessel with one half of the exterior painted in complex opposed red and black designs and the other half painted with a series of paired, ticked, thin black lines without solid red or black elements. The small bowl is painted on the interior with a simple quartered design; the exterior is undecorated. The Villa Ahumada Polychrome jar (Vessel 57; Fig. 2.18f) is small with two loop handles or suspension lugs just below the rim. The exterior is decorated with a band of opposed red and black triangles and interlocking frets. The short neck, which is slightly everted, is decorated with a checkerboard band. The final Chihuahua vessel (Vessel 56; Fig. 2.18c) is another human effigy that has been extensively and badly restored and repainted. It is probably a Ramos Polychrome jar, but in its present condition it is impossible to tell.

Vessels of the Chihuahua polychromes are rare in Salado whole vessel collections. The 1974 surface collections recovered very small amounts of Ramos Polychrome and undifferentiated Chihuahua polychromes. It is therefore curious that Fortenberry and Bennett (1968) note almost the entire Chihuahua polychrome series, including Babicora Polychrome, Carretas Polychrome, Dublan Polychrome, Huerigos Polychrome, as well as Villa Ahumada Polychrome and Ramos Polychrome.

El Paso Polychrome Vessels

The second most frequent decorated type in the 1974 surface collections, El Paso Polychrome (Fig. 2.19a–e) represented about 2 percent of the entire sample. In the whole vessel collection, El Paso Polychrome pottery includes two bowls and five jars (three illustrated). The two bowls (Vessels 32, 52; Fig. 2.19c, e) are painted on the interior only; Vessel 32 has a kill hole and was in a burial association with Gila Polychrome (Table 2.6, Context B). The five jars are of two shapes: spherical bodies with sharply everted rims and ovoid bodies with longer necks and direct (or very slightly everted) rims. Vessels with sharply everted rims include two small jars (Vessels 25, 43; Fig. 2.19b, d) and one large jar (Vessel X–4). The two small jars appear to have band designs of opposed "terraces" running around the middle of the body (Vessel 43) or on the vessel upper half and shoulder (Vessel 25). Jar 25 is a cremation urn (Table 2.6, Context F). The large everted rim jar (Vessel X–4) has a band of complexly interlocked frets on the upper body, shoulder, and lower neck. The two direct-rim jars include one large jar (Vessel 18; Fig. 2.19a) with sharp shoulder and a band design of complex interlocked frets from the shoulder to just below the rim and a small jar

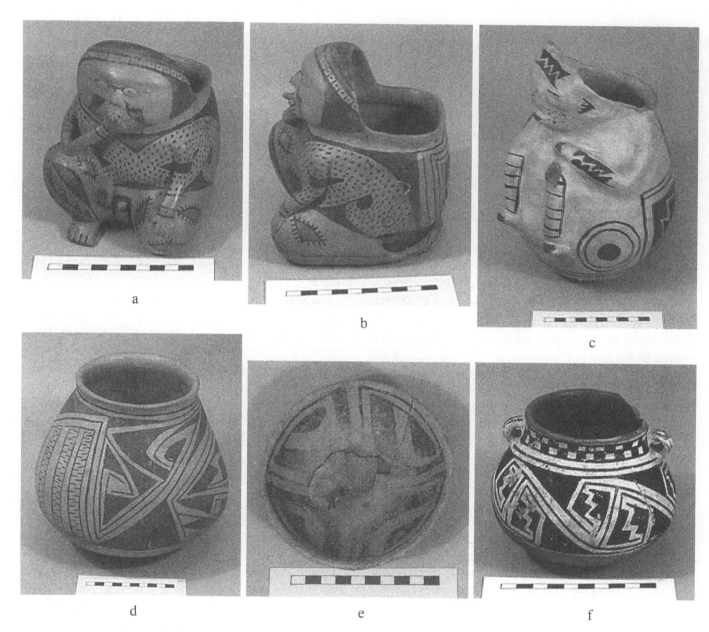

Figure 2.18. Ramos Polychrome vessels (*a–e*) and a Villa Ahumada Polychrome jar (*f*).
Table 2.3 Vessel No.: *a, b* (side view), 10; *c,* 56; *d,* 9; *e,* 71; *f,* 57. (Scale in cm.)

(Vessel X–2) with an indistinguishable design on the upper half of the body.

Chupadero Black-on-white Vessels

Three small (Vessels 6, 16, 53; Fig. 2.19*f, g, i*) and one large (Vessel 21; Fig. 2.19*h*) Chupadero Black-on-white pitchers have round bodies, short narrow necks with slightly everted rims, and a single round or strap handle from the upper body to the rim. All four have the characteristic flat bottom of that type, but three appear smaller than "typical" Chupadero jars. Only Vessel 21 approaches the 30-cm diameter described as "almost standard" for Chupadero pitchers and jars (Hayes and others 1981: 70). Vessel 53 was associated with Gila Polychrome (Table 2.6, Context A) and Vessel 6 with Gila Polychrome and Ramos Polychrome (Table 2.6, Context D). Chupadero Black-on-white pottery began in the late twelfth century and extended through the fourteenth and into the early fifteenth century. Chupadero Black-on-white vessels at Dutch Ruin appear, stylistically, to belong to the early portion of that time range.

Figure 2.19. El Paso Polychrome vessels (*a–e*), and Chupadero Black-on-white pitchers (*f–i*). Table 2.3 Vessel No.: *a*, 18; *b*, 25; *c*, 32; *d*, 43; *e*, 52; *f*, 6; *g*, 16; *h*, 21; *i*, 53. (Scale in cm.)

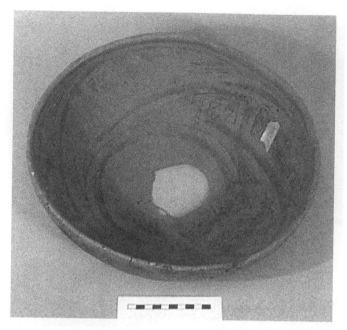

Figure 2.20. White Mountain Red Ware bowl. Table 2.3 Vessel 59. (Scale in cm.)

Figure 2.21. Mesa Verde style mug. Table 2.3 Vessel 68. (Scale in cm.)

White Mountain Red Ware Bowl

Two bowls represent White Mountain Red Ware in the whole vessel collection. One large bowl (Vessel 59; Fig. 2.20) is badly preserved and heavily restored; it could be almost any of the late White Mountain types; most likely it is Wingate Black-on-red. Preservation was sufficiently poor that it is possible that white paint on the exterior may have disappeared. The bowl has a kill hole. The other vessel (X–5) is a large, classic St. Johns Polychrome bowl that is no longer in the Johnson-Humrickhouse collections. The context of this vessel is unknown.

Mesa Verde or Magdalena Black-on-white Mug

A badly restored Mesa Verde-style mug (Vessel 68; Fig. 2.21) may be McElmo, Mesa Verde, or Magdalena Black-on-white. This piece seems far from home. It is possible that this vessel was not found at Dutch Ruin, but since sources for this pottery existed much closer than the Four Corners, it may not be as out-of-place as it seems.

Cibola White Ware Vessels

The only Cibola White Ware ceramics represented in the whole vessel collection are one small Red Mesa Black-on-white pitcher (Vessel 67; Fig. 2.22*a*) and two ladles or scoops of unknown type (Vessels 72, 73; Fig. 2.22*b*, *c*).

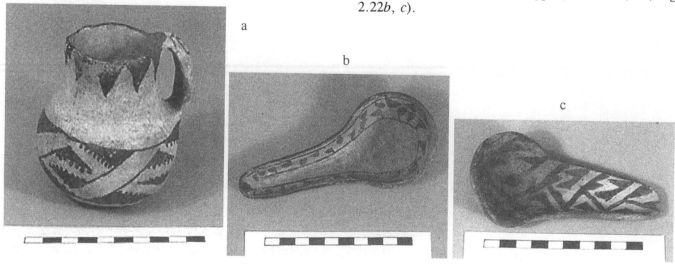

a

b

c

Figure 2.23. Mimbres White Wares. Table 2.3 Vessel No.: *a*, 14 (Style III); *b*, 28 (Style II–III); *c*, 46 (Style II); *d*, 74 (Style I). (Scale in cm.)

Mimbres White Ware Vessels

Two scoops and three small bowls are Mimbres White Ware. The scoops display Mimbres Style I (Vessel 74; Fig. 2.23*d*) and Mimbres Style II (Vessel 46; Fig. 2.23*c*) designs. The small bowls include a Mimbres Style I fragment (Vessel X–1), a Style II-III bowl (Vessel 28; Fig. 2.23*b*), and a Style III bowl (Vessel 14; Fig. 2.23*a*). Neither of the last two are "classic" Mimbres Style III. The five vessels represent an early Mimbres component. Two other vessels "found on a Mimbres floor" and assigned to an "early Mimbres component" are a brown ware effigy jar fragment (X–6) and an Alma Scored(?) bowl (Vessel 17; Fig. 2.10*f*) that was associated with the small Mimbres II–III bowl (Vessel 28; Fig. 2.23*b*; Table 2.6, Context E). These vessels are mostly miniatures, ladles, and effigies, forms that might be differentially curated by succeeding generations.

←

Figure 2.22. Cibola White Ware vessels. Table 2.3 Vessel No.: *a*, 67 (Red Mesa Black-on-white); *b*, *c*, 72, 73 (scoops, type unknown). (Scale in cm.)

CONTEXTS AND ASSOCIATIONS

By contrasting and combining notes, catalogue entries, and photographs, it is possible to reconstruct associations and contexts for at least 27 of the 81 vessels in this collection. Pots were noted as having been "found together" and found in particular situations, such as in burials or on floors. Specifically, there are seven groups of associated vessels that represent relatively secure contexts and two more contexts that are less certain (Table 2.6, p. 18).

Three of the contexts (Table 2.6, A, E, and H) represent floor assemblages. Context A is a Salado period assemblage, most likely from Room 3 (but perhaps from Room 6). In Context A, two of the Gila Polychrome vessels (13, 26; Fig. 2.16*c*, *d*) are large jars, one (19; Fig. 2.15*d*) is a small bowl, and the fourth (1; Fig. 2.15*a*) is a "submarine" or "football" shaped vessel. The Chupadero Black-on-white pitcher (Vessel 53; Fig. 2.19*i*) is small, but not a miniature. The Tucson Polychrome bowl (Vessel X–10) and the corrugated jar (Vessel 36; Fig. 2.13*f*) are both full-sized and otherwise unexceptional. None of these vessels have kill holes, which supports their attribution to a floor 01 assemblage rather than a burial. Context E consists of two brown ware vessels (Vessels 17, X–6; Fig. 2.10*f*) and a miniature Mimbres Style II–III bowl (Vessel 28; Fig. 2.23*b*), "found on a Mimbres floor"; no details are available about the location of the Mimbres floor, but it may have been beneath the excavated Salado rooms. Context H may be spurious; both vessels (a plain brown jar (Vessel 45; Fig. 2.10*g*) and a red-slipped corrugated jar (Vessel 54; Fig. 2.13*i*) were found on floors, and there is a suggestion that both were on the floor of Room 6.

Three groups (Table 2.6, Contexts B, C, D) represent mortuary vessels from inhumations and Context F and Context G are cremation vessels. (For an excellent review of mortuary data from the Upper Gila and adjacent regions, see Woodson and others 1999.) It is likely that many of the vessels that could not be assigned to contexts or associations because they lacked provenience are also from burials or cremations, but these five contexts represent those vessels for which information in notes or photographs is available. The three inhumation groups vary from two to five vessels. Context D was definitely associated with a subfloor inhumation, probably adult. The group consists of two Ramos jars (Vessel 9, Fig. 2.18*d*, and Vessel 10, Fig. 2.18*a*, *b*, two views), two Gila Polychrome bowls (Vessels 2, 27; Fig. 2.15*b*, Fig. 2.16*e*) and one Chupadero Black-on-white pitcher (Vessel 6, Fig. 2.19*f*). One Gila Polychrome bowl (Vessel 27) is definitely associated with this burial; it has a kill hole. The other Gila Polychrome bowl (Vessel 2; Fig. 2.15*b*) is only tentatively assigned to this group.

In contrast to kill holes, Chihuahua polychrome jars associated with burials at Paquime often had distinctive paired "suspension" holes or perforations on opposite sides of the vessel rim or paired perforated lugs. Most vessels with burials did not have these features; most vessels *with* these features were with burials (Di Peso and others 1974b, Fig. 370–8). The association of these features with burials at Paquime was so strong as to suggest that "vessels with lugs or perforations were specifically manufactured as funeral furniture" (Di Peso and others 1974b: 365). Intriguingly, neither of the Chihuahua polychromes with Context D has either holes or lugs. Indeed, few vessels at Dutch Ruin have these features, except for (1) a small brown ware jar (Vessel 33; Fig. 2.10*d*) in Context B associated with Gila Polychrome and El Paso Polychrome, and (2) a Villa Ahumada Polychrome jar (57; Fig. 2.18*f*) of unknown context.

The vessels in Context B were "found together," but were less positively associated with a subfloor inhumation. Context B includes two Gila Polychrome bowls (Vessels 3, 4; Fig. 2.15*c*, 2.16*a*), an El Paso Polychrome bowl (32; Fig. 2.19*c*), and a brown ware jar (33; Fig. 2.10*d*) containing beads. Two of the bowls (4, 32) have kill holes. Vessels in Context C were also "found together," but were less definitely associated with a subfloor inhumation: one corrugated exterior bowl with a smudged polished interior (5; Fig. 2.12) and one Playas Red Tooled bowl (15; Fig. 2.13*b*) with a kill hole.

Context F and Context G (Table 2.6) are subfloor cremation vessels. Context F consists of an El Paso Polychrome jar (25; Fig. 2.19*b*) used as a cremation urn and a Tucson Polychrome bowl (24; Fig. 2.17*b*) inverted over the jar. Context G is a single vessel, a red-slipped tooled jar (22; Fig. 2.13*d*) used as a cremation urn, without an identified "covering bowl."

The vessel in Context I is a Mimbres Style III Black-on-white bowl (14; Fig. 2.23*a*) that was described as an inverted "cover bowl over bead jar." From various lines of evidence, it appears likely that the "bead jar" was not Vessel 33, the brown ware jar with otolith beads in Context B, so there must be another vessel in the collection that is the "bead jar." No further information is available; we do not know if the bowl was on a floor, or subfloor, or in another context altogether.

It is likely that many and perhaps most of the other Dutch Ruin vessels come from burial contexts. To explain why this might be so requires a brief digression into the composition of the collection. The vessel forms and wares represented by the Dutch Ruin whole vessels appear to be biased in favor of painted and decorated types. "Utility" types are underrepresented in the Johnson-Humrickhouse collection, with only 15 corrugated, plain, or textured vessels representing about 20 percent of the collection. Playas Red would add 8 more vessels to that total, if it is considered a utility type. Dutch Ruin whole vessels show a ratio of about 4.5:1 painted to nonpainted vessels contrasted to the 1974 systematic surface collections that produced a ratio of about 0.25:1 painted to nonpainted sherds from the site. In many and probably most southwestern assemblages, utility bowls and jars significantly outnumber painted and decorated vessels, as, for example, at Salado sites in the Cliff Valley (Wallace 1998) and in the Mimbres Valley (Nelson and LeBlanc 1986).

The composition of the Dutch Ruin collection may partly reflect differential reconstruction of decorated vessels as opposed to utility vessels by Fortenberry and Bennett. But it is also plausible that the whole vessel collections disproportionately reflect burial contexts, where utility, and especially large utility, vessels would presumably be infrequent. Only six vessels can be definitely assigned and five probably assigned to inhumations, and only three vessels are definitely assigned to cremations. Twelve vessels are from floor assemblages (Table 2.6), and sketch maps suggest perhaps five more vessels were found on floors.

It is likely that many of the remaining 50 vessels without known specific provenience also come from burials. There are a remarkable number of vessels with kill holes, and these vessels are all bowls (Table 2.5). Recall that kill holes are small holes punched out of the base of bowls, most familiar from Mimbres burial practices. At Dutch Ruin, four bowls definitely or likely associated with inhumations show kill holes and a number of vessels presumably from burials show this same modification. Of 40 bowls, 17 have kill holes (Table 2.5). None of these bowls are Mimbres white wares; in fact the vessels most frequently modified in this way are of the Salado type, Gila Polychrome, with kill holes in 10 of 16 bowls. One Tonto Polychrome bowl, another Salado type, contains a kill hole. The next most frequent is Tucson Polychrome, with 3 of 7 bowls so modified. Other vessels with kill holes include St. Johns Polychrome, El Paso Polychrome, Playas Red, and plain brown bowls. Four bowls with kill holes are definitely associated with inhumations; neither of the documented cremations includes killed vessels (Table 2.6, Contexts F and G). It is highly likely that the 13 killed vessels with nonspecific proveniences were originally associated with burials, either inhumations or cremations.

There was no indication of extramural burials or cemeteries at Dutch Ruin, and I believe that the 12 (at least) intramural inhumations and the five intramural cremations reflect the actual total number of inhumations and cremations excavated by Fortenberry and Bennett. All three of the documented inhumations contained killed bowls but, as noted, the two cremations did not. Cremations in the Upper Gila are often contained in a single bowl or jar, or a cover bowl-jar set. At the Ormand site near Cliff, New Mexico, of almost 70 vessels associated with cremations, only "several had kill holes" according to Wallace (1998: 170); an exact number is unavailable. If the remaining three cremations at Dutch Ruin had one killed bowl each, that leaves 10 killed bowls unaccounted for. It seems statistically probable that at least some and perhaps as many as 10 of the 13 killed vessels with no specific provenience were found with some or all of the nine inhumations for which we have no data. If so, this would constitute an exception to the larger patterning of killed vessels at Salado sites and to previous conclusions about the final use and function of Salado polychromes at Upper Gila sites.

Patricia Crown summarized the distribution of Salado polychromes with kill holes, reporting 10 sites that had "definite killed vessels": Hawikuh, Kinishba, Los Muertos, AZ W:10:50 (ASM) at Point of Pines, Gila Bank Ruin, Ormand Village, Buena Vista, Second Canyon, Kuykendall, and Slaughter Ranch. "Killed vessels occur most often with cremated remains (only four killed vessels were found with inhumations; three from the Gila Bank Ruin and one from Kinishba)" (Crown 1994: 108). At Dutch Ruin, Salado polychromes (Gila Polychrome and the one Tonto Polychrome) constitute 10 of the 17 killed bowls. The situation at Dutch Ruin, then, where killed bowls apparently are associated with inhumations, runs counter to the widespread pattern observed by Crown.

Similarly, the association of Gila Polychrome with burials (either inhumations or cremations) contradicts the general pattern of Salado polychrome vessels in the Upper Gila being found on floors and not in burials (Lekson 2000). But not at Dutch Ruin: if kill holes may be taken as a reasonably certain indication of mortuary association (based on earlier Mimbres practices), then at least 10 of the 21 Gila Polychrome vessels (16 bowls, 4 jars, and 1 "submarine" vessel) were burial furniture. At least four Gila Polychrome vessels were found on a room floor (Table 2.6, Context A), but clearly, my earlier generalization about the context of Salado polychromes does not apply at the Dutch Ruin, although the pattern may be true at other Upper Gila sites.

In summary, whole vessels from the Dutch Ruin collections come primarily from floor assemblages or burial lots. The floor assemblages include two or more multiple-vessel floor groups (Table 2.6, Contexts A, E, H), plus at least four to six individual vessels shown on floors on the site map, for a total of at least 16 to 18 vessels. Fourteen vessels are thought to be associated with inhumations or cremations (Table 2.6, Contexts B, C, D, F, and G). Together, these vessels account for less than half of the Dutch Ruin collection.

No bowls in floor groups (Table 2.6, Contexts A, E, H) have kill holes. Of seven bowls with three inhumations (Table 2.6, Contexts B, C, D), four have kill holes and three do not (that is, half have kill holes). Only one bowl was found with a cremation (Context F), and it does not have a kill hole.

Twenty-one inhumations are indicated on the site map, plus the annotation "ten or more" in Room 10 (of which Contexts B, C, and D comprise only three). The map indicates at least seven subfloor cremations (of which Contexts F and Context G comprise two).

Thirteen of the 25 bowls with kill holes that were *not* assigned to burial groups (Table 2.6, Contexts B, C, D, F, and G) or floor assemblages (Table 2.6, Contexts A, E, and H, none of which had kill holes) include Vessels 7, 29, 30, 31, 38, 39, 41, 44, 49, 50, 59, 61, X–8), slightly more than half of the unassigned bowls; if the proportions of four killed and three non-killed bowls (from inhumation contexts B, C, and D) hold, it could be argued that many and probably most of the unassigned bowls with *and* without kill holes came from the 20 to 30 inhumations. The three inhumations (Table 2.6, Contexts B, C, D) included three jars and a pitcher; extrapolating to 20 inhumations, many of the 20 jars *not* assigned to floor assemblages or burial groups might also be included in inhumation contexts.

The five cremations for which we have no ceramic data might also account for five jars, and several more bowls (with or without kill holes) could have been covering bowls for those cremations. Additionally, the Villa Ahumada Polychrome jar (Vessel 57) had lugs, a vessel feature associated with burials at Paquime. Although this vessel has no clear context or association, it is possible and even probable that it, too, was burial furniture.

In conclusion, although it cannot be documented because there is no positive context information, it is highly likely that almost all but about five vessels (representing vessels noted as found on floors) came from the 20 to 30 inhumations and 5 cremations for which we currently have no ceramic data. It is now impossible to determine which five pots were found on floors, but it is plausible that all 13 bowls with kill holes and perhaps the Villa Ahumada Polychrome jar with lugs were burial furniture, and an argument can be made that most or almost all of the remaining vessels were grave goods also.

COMPARABLE COLLECTIONS

There are several whole vessel collections from other Upper Gila Salado sites (Fig. 1.1). These collections are variable in recovery, presentation, and accessibility, but they provide useful comparisons for the evaluation of the Dutch Ruin collection. In this section, the Dutch Ruin whole vessel collection is briefly compared with collections from the Solomonsville, Dinwiddie, and Ormand sites. Sherd data from Dutch Ruin are contrasted with other more-or-less systematic collections from the Ormand, Willow Creek, and Villareal II sites and with type lists from other sites. The description of decorated or painted pottery is terminologically consistent across these several sites, using the conventional Southwestern bino-

mial typology; plain and textured wares, however, are described quite differently from site to site. Therefore, these brief discussions of each site emphasize decorated types and assume that the application of the typology was roughly comparable from site to site (and analyst to analyst).

Several different whole vessel collections are available from the Solomonsville site (aka Buena Vista, Curtis Site, Pueblo Viejo) near Safford, Arizona. Solomonsville is one of the largest and most important sites on the Upper Gila and spans (minimally) the tenth through fourteenth centuries. It includes many room blocks of both adobe and stone masonry, a huge Hohokam ball court, and earlier pit house components of both Hohokam and Mimbres affiliation (see Tyberg 2000).

Two major excavations at Solomonsville produced large whole vessel collections: Oscar Tatman's work in 1931 (Brown 1973; Tyberg 2000) and Jack and Vera Mills' excavations in the 1970s (Mills and Mills 1978). The Tatman collections are at the University Museum at the University of Colorado, Boulder; the Mills' collections were formerly housed at the museum of Eastern Arizona Community College in Thatcher, Arizona, but their current location is uncertain.

The two collections are somewhat complementary: Tatman worked entirely within room blocks, finding vessels on floors and in subfloor inhumations. The Mills excavated in room blocks but the whole vessel data are not available for floor contexts. Reasonably accurate data are available from the Mills' excavation of subfloor inhumation burials and extramural cemeteries. Thus the two collections provide whole vessel assemblages from rooms floors, intramural inhumations (and a few cremations), and extramural cremations.

Within room blocks, Tatman's excavations produced 118 whole or partial vessels now in the University of Colorado museum collections (Brown 1973; Tyberg 2000), of which 76 came from nonburial contexts. The nonburial whole vessels were approximately evenly divided between plain or textured (39) and decorated (37) vessels. The decorated vessels are almost exclusively Salado polychromes, except for two Tucson or Maverick Mountain Polychrome vessels. The extensive excavations by Mills and Mills (1978) in Solomonsville room blocks undoubtedly produced a comparable collection, but no accurate numerical information can be reconstructed from the report, and their collections are no longer available for study

Tatman (Tyberg 2000) and Mills and Mills (1978) excavated about 100 subfloor inhumations at Solomonsville; associated ceramics consisted of at least 34 plain or textured vessels, 26 Salado polychrome vessels and a Maverick Mountain Polychrome vessel. Almost 80 percent of these subfloor inhumations were infants or young children. A total of six subfloor cremations (both infants and adults) included four brown ware vessels, one black-on-white jar, and one Salado polychrome jar.

Excavations at a cremation cemetery area at Solomonsville produced 60 vessels (Mills and Mills 1978: 65–85), of which more than half were plain or textured, approximately 20 percent were red-on-brown, and the remainder were various black-on-red and polychromes (St. Johns Polychrome, Tucson Polychrome, Kwakina Polychrome), notably *excluding* Salado types. The low proportion of painted types other than red-on-brown in Solomonsville cremations, both intra- and extramural is striking and is addressed in later discussions.

Although no systematic sherd sample is available from Solomonsville, Tyberg (2000, Table 4–3) lists types present in Tatman's collection of 919 sherds, of which 656 were painted. Painted sherds represent some 35 types, comparable in variety to the Dutch Ruin. However, Solomonsville is clearly multicomponent, with earlier Mimbres and Sedentary period Hohokam features. Mimbres ceramics included three decorated types; Hohokam ceramics included six different types. Thus the total number of types representing the Salado component at Solomonsville is about 25, approximately the same as the Salado period types at the Dutch Ruin.

The Dinwiddie Site, on Duck Creek near Cliff, New Mexico, was excavated by Jack and Vera Mills from 1966 to 1970 (Mills and Mills 1972). The report is useful but incomplete. It was a large fourteenth-century adobe pueblo and the Mills excavated about 30 rooms in it. Other large Salado sites exist on Duck Creek, but none have been systematically investigated (Lekson 1992b, 2000).

All whole or partial vessels from Dinwiddie are apparently from floor or floor fill contexts (that is, there were few if any intramural subfloor burials), and little work was done in extramural areas. The exact number of whole or partial vessels is difficult to determine, but from the report it appears to have been at least 80; of these about 36 are decorated and include Gila, Tonto, Tucson, and El Paso polychromes (Mills and Mills 1972: 48). No systematic sherd samples are available, although it might be possible to compile sherd data from the report.

The Salado component of the Ormand Site (LA 5793), near Cliff, New Mexico, consists of four adobe room blocks, a separate ceremonial chamber, and at least two cemeteries (Dittert 1966; Wallace 1998). Wallace (1998: 412) dates Ormand from about A.D. 1300 to perhaps the early 1400s. Dean Wilson (in Wallace 1998: 195–285) analyzed 23,805 sherds and 83 whole or partial vessels from Ormand. In the whole vessel assemblage almost half of the vessels were "brown utility wares," in marked contrast to the Dutch Ruin assemblage where "utility wares" constituted only one-fifth of the collection.

This difference may reflect extensive cremation cemeteries at Ormand. The cremation burials at Dutch Ruin (Table 2.6, Contexts F and G) were contained in and accompanied by only nonpainted pottery; a pattern also characterizing Solomonsville where painted and decorated pottery other than red-on-brown was rare in cremations. At Ormand, almost 40 cremations were recovered in the cemetery, accompanied by 28 plain or textured vessels and only 6 decorated vessels. It appears that cremation burials were associated with proportionately far fewer painted and decorated vessels than were inhumations, and thus the large number of cremations excavated contributes to the difference in proportions of painted to nonpainted whole vessels between Ormand and Dutch Ruin.

The almost 3,000 decorated sherds from Ormand represented 14 types, of which four or five were associated with an earlier Late Pit House period or Mangas phase component. Thus, the Salado decorated ceramics at Ormand represent about 10 types, or about half the number represented at the Dutch Ruin.

The Willow Creek site (Fitting 1973), located in the Magus Creek drainage on the north flanks of the Big Burro Mountains, is a large Salado site with about 80 rooms in two separate room blocks and an undefined earlier Mimbres component represented by sherds. Limited testing produced a ceramic sample of just over 3,000 sherds, of which 330 were painted. The painted sherds represented only four types, of which two were in Mimbres series. Indeed, the only Salado period decorated types were Gila Polychrome and Tonto Polychrome.

Smaller excavated fourteenth-century Salado sites in the Upper Gila produced few whole vessels. Villareal II (Chapter 3) produced three nonpainted partial vessels; Riverside Ruin (Baker 1971) produced one partial Gila Polychrome bowl from a room floor. The ceramic sherd assemblage at Villareal II was slightly more varied than Willow Creek, with 8 to 10 Salado period decorated types represented, including Gila, Tonto, Tucson, and El Paso polychromes. Riverside was more limited, with only two Salado period decorated vessels (Baker 1971).

Perhaps the most famous Upper Gila Salado site is Kwilleylekia (LA 8674; Fig. 1.1*b*). Unfortunately, the large whole vessel collections from Kwilleylekia appear to have been dispersed. Richard Ellison reported to me in 1974 that there was a broad range of late fourteenth-century and early fifteenth-century pottery at the site, which he dated from about A.D. 1415 to 1575, much later than the other sites mentioned here and far later than most archaeologists would extend Salado polychromes, of which both Gila Polychrome and Tonto Polychrome were abundant at the site.

DATING

The whole vessel collections from Dutch Ruin and the surface ceramics from the 1974 survey are divided into two general groups: Mimbres and Salado. The Mimbres vessels appear to date typologically from the twelfth century, although earlier sherds were present in both surface and excavated samples. The majority of the pottery in the vessel collection appears to date to fourteenth-century Salado assemblages.

The Chupadero Black-on-white vessels probably date to the early half of that type's long duration, which extended from the late twelfth through the early sixteenth century (Hayes and others 1981: 67–73); they would not be out of place with late Mimbres or Black Mountain assemblages but also could appear in Salado assemblages. El Paso Polychrome is almost equally long-lived; the direct rim of Vessel 18 (Fig. 2.19*a*) suggests an early date in that span, whereas the distinctly everted rims of the remaining El Paso Polychrome jars suggest a later placement, in the fourteenth century or even fifteenth century (Whalen 1985).

St. Johns Polychrome (represented by bowl X–5, of unknown context) began in the late twelfth century and continued through the thirteenth century and perhaps into the early fourteenth century (Kintigh 1996). Gila Polychrome is now generally agreed to date late in the thirteenth century and more likely into the fourteenth century (Crown 1994). Tucson Polychrome is considered a fourteenth century type (Lindsay 1992). Mesa Verde or Magdalena Black-on-white, if indeed present, is associated elsewhere with fourteenth-century types. The Chihuahua polychromes at Dutch Ruin almost certainly date to the fourteenth century (following the revised dating of Dean and Ravesloot 1993); other wares often assumed to be Chihuahuan (such as red-slipped plain wares) may begin earlier.

The dating of Dutch Ruin may be complicated by recent remarks made by Ben Nelson (2000: 323), suggesting:

(1) Chihuahuan pottery in association with Mimbres pottery in the Mimbres Valley and the Black Range; (2) Chihuahuan pottery with Reserve wares and without Mimbres Black-on-white or Gila Polychrome in the Mimbres Valley and Cliff area.

These statements perplexed more than a few archaeologists, since they seemed to imply Casas Grandes series pottery in the eleventh and twelfth centuries, centuries before Paquime (see also LeBlanc and Nelson 1976; Nelson and LeBlanc 1986). A recent volume on late Mimbres archaeology of the Black Range specifically notes that "Postclassic" post-Mimbres sites have no "Chihuahuan types" (Nelson 1999: 182), and a synthesis of ceramic assemblages from southwestern New Mexico (Lekson 1992b) failed to note any associations of Mimbres or Reserve black-on-whites with Chihuahua polychrome ceramics.

Communication with Ben Nelson on 23 August 2000 largely clarified this situation: by "Chihuahuan ceramics" he referred not to painted types or to polychromes, but to Playas red wares. Although it has long been known that Playas red wares are found in association with late Mimbres and, less often, Reserve assemblages, many archaeologists question whether all types or varieties subsumed under the rubric Playas Red are indeed manufactured in the Casas Grandes region or associated with Paquime (for example, Wiseman 1981). "Playas Red" appears to be a long-lived group of types or wares that were made in different areas at different times. Playas Red was an important ware at Paquime, but so too was El Paso Polychrome, which (like Playas) was made in other areas as early as the late twelfth century. In summary, Nelson was *not* arguing for Chihuahua polychromes in association with pre-1300 assemblages in the Upper Gila or at other sites in southwestern New Mexico.

Finally, late "Rio Grande Glaze D or E" sherds noted by Fortenberry and Bennett (1968) would not necessarily be out of place: Kwilleylekia in the Cliff Valley may have lasted that late in time, but late Rio Grande glazes seem incompatible with the remainder of the sherd and whole vessel collections; some misidentification by Fortenberry and Bennett is possible.

CHAPTER THREE

Villareal II

Villareal II (LA 34794), a small multicomponent site in the Cliff Valley (see Fig. 1.1), was named for the old Villareal ranch on which it was located. The ruin was visited and mapped by Harriett and C. B. Cosgrove (1929), who noted a "circle of stones, 4 [feet] in diameter" in the area south of the room block; this feature was not evident in 1972. The Cosgroves called the site "Ruin 3, Villareal Ranch."

The site is located on a dissected terrace bench just above the confluence of Garcia Canyon and the Gila River, on the left (east) bank of the river, about 3.4 km (2.1 miles) north of the town of Gila, New Mexico (see Fig. 1.5). In the early 1970s, the land was owned by the Pacific Western Land and Cattle Company, which graciously allowed archaeological research. The site was designated G–19 during a survey made by James E. Fitting in 1971 and 1972. Fitting's survey revealed a series of four sites (G–18 through G–21) that were designated Villareal I through IV (Appendix A). Villareal I was partially excavated by the Chippewa Nature Center under the direction of Fel Brunnett in 1973 and 1974. I mapped and tested Villareal III and IV in 1973 (Appendix A).

In the summer of 1972 Villareal II was excavated as part of the Upper Gila Project, under the overall direction of James E. Fitting; Timothy C. Klinger and I served as field directors and we published a brief preliminary account of the 1972 season (Lekson and Klinger 1973). The rest of the crew consisted of Betsy Skinner, Linda Brown, Liz Horenstein, and Ken Robbie. Klinger analyzed the ceramics and Skinner analyzed the lithics. Excavations took place from July 8 to July 29. A small crew spent three days at the site in 1973 and conducted systematic surface collections and excavated Test Pit 1. All measurements in excavations and field operations were made in feet and inches; I follow that system in publishing this field data with the addition of approximate metric equivalencies when deemed helpful for comparisons with other reports.

Villareal II (Fig. 3.1) consisted of a room block with five rooms and an isolated room (Unit A). Two cobble features (B and C in Fig. 3.1) and two check dams constituted the other structural features visible from the surface at the site. Two pit houses were located beneath the main room block, and an extensive surface scatter of lithic and ceramic materials was associated with the site.

Prior to excavation, the main room block was a low mound, rising about 1.5 feet (46 cm) above the surrounding ground surface (Fig. 3.1). Very little rubble was visible on the surface of the mound, but parts of the east wall of Room 3 and the west walls of Rooms 1 and 4 were clearly visible as cimientos, two or three parallel rows of small, upright river cobbles (also called "footing stones," Nelson and LeBlanc 1986) forming the bases of puddled adobe walls. Several disturbances, probably potholes, were noted.

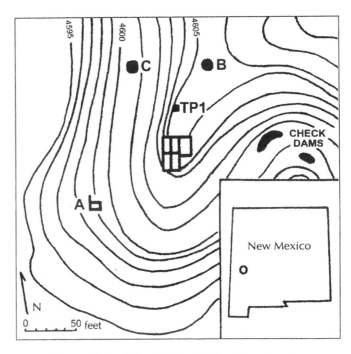

Figure 3.1. The Villareal II site, showing location of Test Pit 1, isolated room Unit A, two surface cobble features (B, C), and check dams.

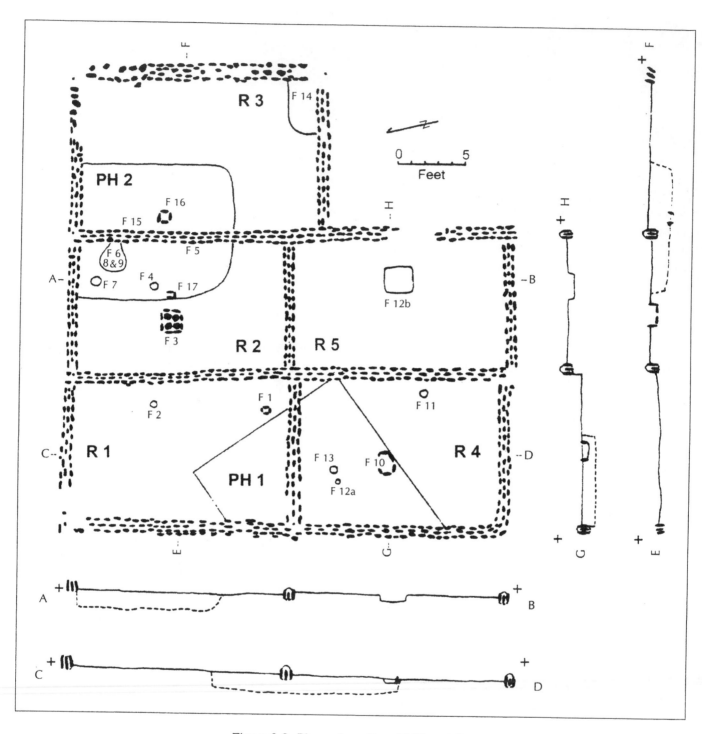

Figure 3.2. Plan and profiles of Villareal II.

Excavators outlined both sides of each wall with trenches (1 foot wide, 4 to 6 inches deep, 30–by–10 cm; Fig. 3.2). Trench fill was retained and screened with the appropriate room fill. Following the definition of walls, a steel spike was fixed at the mutual corner of Rooms 1, 2, 4, and 5 (the highest point on the site).

This spike served as a vertical datum for all excavations in the main room block and additional spikes at every corner provided horizontal control. All mapping was coordinated by tape triangulation within this system of fixed points. A separate vertical datum was established at the southwest corner of the room comprising Unit A.

Excavations began in Room 1 and continued in sequence. Room 1 was excavated in arbitrary 6-inch (15 cm) levels, but when it became apparent that the depth to floor was very shallow, we discontinued using arbitrary levels in room fill. Excavation in Rooms 2 through 5 and in Pit Houses 1 and 2 proceeded as follows: first, a small test (usually about 1.5-by-1.5 feet square, 46-by-46 cm) was made to determine the depth to floor. The location of this test in each room varied. The fill from this test was treated as room fill. Second, the fill to within about 4 inches (10 cm) of the floor level was removed with mattocks and shovels. Third, the remaining fill, designated "floor fill" was removed with trowels. Materials in contact with the floor, or less than an inch above the floor, were removed and bagged separately as "floor" materials. Fourth, the floor was swept and floor features were defined and excavated. Material from features was bagged separately with a feature provenience; however, there was no finer internal provenience within features, except unintentionally in the case of Features 6, 8, and 9 (see Room 2, below). Fill from Features 3, 5 through 10, 12B, 13, and 16 represented in situ deposits. Other contexts were either sterile or fill of postoccupational origin. Features were numbered sequentially across the site, but *not* within individual rooms. The designation "feature" was intended to represent a discrete depositional or architectural unit smaller than a "room"; however, Feature 5 was a vessel fragment on the floor of Room 2. Feature number 12 was accidentally assigned twice, and letter suffixes "A" and "B" were added to distinguish the two units.

After the excavation of floors and features, subfloor tests were made in corners, along walls, and in the centers of rooms. If undisturbed soil was encountered, the tests were discontinued. Pit Houses 1 and 2 appeared beneath Rooms 1, 2, 3, and 4. These units were defined after removing the room floors above them and were then excavated following the room procedures.

All fill, floor fill, and feature fill was screened through ¼-inch mesh hardware cloth. Samples of ashy soil from firepits were retained for botanical analysis; however, no samples were collected from room floors or from any fill deposits. A single sample for ^{14}C dating was recovered from the fill of Pit House 1.

ARCHITECTURE AND STRATIGRAPHY

The architecture and stratigraphy of Villareal II were relatively simple (Fig. 3.2). The site consisted of a compact room block of five adobe-walled rooms superimposed over two rectangular semisubterranean pit houses, an isolated masonry room, an extensive surface artifact scatter, two check dams, and two undefined small cobble features. The term "northeast surface concentration" refers to a concentration of material in the surface artifact scatter located about 300 feet (100 m) northeast of the room block.

The room block (Fig. 3.2) consisted of a compact, subrectangular block of five rooms, oriented slightly east-of-north off the cardinal directions. Walls of the room block were preserved as stubs no more than 1.5 feet (43 cm) in height (Fig. 3.3). Wall construction was of puddled adobe, with a basal reinforcement of parallel rows of upright river cobbles or cimientos. These cobbles were generally less than 10 inches high, about 4 inches wide, and less than 3 inches thick (25-by-10-by-7 cm). They had been set in shallow trenches filled with puddled adobe mud, apparently of local origin, with the bases of the stones resting on the bases of the trenches. Most walls had three parallel rows of cobbles, but the east and west exterior walls of the block had four rows in limited sections. Few additional masonry stones or cobbles were recovered in the excavation of room fill, and it appears that walls above the cimientos were of puddled adobe or perishable materials. North-south walls were continuous and presumably were built first. East-west walls had been added later and they abutted the north-south walls, a configuration that seemingly denotes three possible construction units: (1) Rooms 1 and 4, (2) Rooms 2 and 5, and (3) Room 3. However, there is no evidence to show that any appreciable length of time passed between the construction of any two units. Probably all five rooms were built within a short period of time and perhaps in a single event.

In isolated places in Rooms 4 and 5, a tan clay plaster covered the basal cobble cimientos and coarser adobe of the walls on the interior faces of the rooms. Absence of wall plaster in Rooms 1, 2, and 3 may be a function of preservation, but standing wall heights of the common walls of Rooms 1 and 2 and Rooms 2 and 3 were equal to those of the walls in Rooms 4 and 5 with surviving plaster, and it seems likely if originally present, plaster would have also survived on the walls of these rooms.

Little direct evidence of roofing survived. The fill of all rooms contained abundant, small, weathered fragments of adobe similar to that observed in the walls. These fragments could represent either roof or wall debris or both. The few postholes were problematic; most of these features were located next to walls and could easily represent storage racks rather than roof supports. Only Room 2 had a central posthole (Feature

Figure 3.3. Room 2 at Villareal II, looking north.

17), and in it were stone wedges or shims, perhaps in-·dicating lateral forces affecting the post and arguing against the interpretation of this posthole as a roof support.

Other postholes associated with the room block (Features 2, 4, and 11) were of questionable function, and in any event no postholes were reinforced for vertical forces directed on roof supports, unless the sterile sand fill and adobe caps of Features 2 and 11 represent an attempt at post seating for vertical loads. It is odd that the adobe cap that supported the putative post (unless the pits had been altered) was not fragmented or crushed in either feature. In the absence of roof support posts, it appears that if the walls were load bearing for the roof, the roof could not have been substantial because the basal width of the walls was only 12 inches (30 cm) at most. An insubstantial roof combined with thin walls would not have provided efficient insulation. It is possible that the adobe walls were not full height and that the upper portions of the walls were built of jacal-type construction with load-bearing uprights seated in the wall above the surviving stubs. However, although adobe fragments were commonly found in room fill, impressions indicating this type of construction were

absent. Feature 1 may have been a posthole, but it is also possible that this feature may instead have been associated with Pit House 1.

Room floors had been thinly plastered with fine clay mud, identical to and occasionally coping into the surviving wall plaster. Floors were differentially preserved. In the well-preserved sections (particularly in the east half of Room 4) the floor was compact and appeared to have been burnished while slightly plastic with a hard tool (perhaps a river cobble). Little cracking was evident, except where floors had settled over subfloor features (particularly over Pit Houses 1 and 2). Floors in Rooms 2, 4, and 5 appeared more level and perhaps more carefully made than those in Rooms 1 and 3. Although erosion on the east and west edges of the mound may have caused differential preservation, the floor of Room 4 on the west edge of the mound was excavated into undisturbed soil and the upper fill of Pit House 1 and leveled, whereas the floor of Room 1, adjacent, was not.

There was some evidence that the floors of Rooms 2 and 3 were laid over leveled surfaces; floor leveling was most marked in Room 4, where this process left the base of the east wall about 8 inches (20 cm) above the

Figure 3.4. Pit House 2, beneath the wall between Rooms 2 and 3 at Villareal II, looking north.

floor level. The floor plaster in Room 4 coped into and continued over the exposed soil face onto the face of the east wall. Apparently the floors were leveled after wall foundations were constructed. It is probably significant that only the leveled floors had fire-pits.

Unit A, an isolated room about 100 feet (30.5 m) southwest of the main room block, was built with a different type of masonry. Double and even triple-wythe river cobbles were set horizontally in abundant mud mortar and remained as wall stubs about 1.5 feet (43 cm) tall above the lowest floor level.

Room fill was full of river cobbles, presumably representing wall rubble, but the amount of rubble in the room fill was not sufficient to raise the surviving stubs to full height. Wall rock may have been "robbed" for later construction, or perhaps these walls were at least partially of puddled adobe or jacal, although no positive evidence of either technique was present. No evidence of roofing remained either, although badly weathered adobe fragments were present in the fill. As in the room fill of the main room block, these fragments could represent the walls, the roof, or both. From surface indications the isolated room northwest of the site appeared to be similar to Unit A, and this room also probably was constructed of multiple cobble horizontally laid masonry.

Two semisubterranean rooms, Pit Houses 1 and 2, were partially excavated (Fig. 3.4). These structures had been truncated by construction of the superimposed rooms, but it is unlikely that either pit house was fully subterranean. Walls must have extended upward around the margins of the rooms, but no direct evidence of these walls remained. Large river cobbles had been tumbled into the fill along one wall of each pit house, and these cobbles may represent razed walls.

A single stone-lined posthole (Feature 1) was perhaps associated with the east wall of Pit House 1. This posthole was located just outside the pit house, at the middle of the east wall. The angle of the posthole was fairly vertical, suggesting that this post may have supported a horizontal beam in the pit house roof. The lack of other postholes along the east wall of the pit house indicates that this post was not a part of jacal wall construction. The west wall of Pit House 1 was not exposed, and in the absence of an opposed post on the west side of Pit House 1, the actual function of the Feature 1 posthole must remain conjectural.

The floors and remaining walls of Pit House 1 were well-plastered, with a clay similar to the floor plaster in the superimposed rooms. The floor of Pit House 2 was also plastered, but the walls showed little evidence of this treatment.

Pit Houses 1 and 2 had been burned and the floor and wall plaster was hardened through heat. Abundant charred vegetal material was found in fill and floor fill. The settling of room floors over these structures indicates that the pit houses may have been burned and intentionally (but only partially) filled shortly before the construction of the main room block, with the fill incompletely compacted.

Room 1

Condition prior to excavation: The mound sloped to the west; the west half of the room was badly eroded, with the west wall clearly visible in several places. The northwest corner of the room was entirely eroded away.

Sequence of excavation: Room 1 was excavated in 6–inch (15 cm) levels, measured from the site datum. The difference in elevation from the southeast corner (location of site datum) and the eroded northwest corner was slightly more than 1 foot; therefore, the third arbitrary level was the first to extend entirely across the room. Following the excavation of Room 1, arbitrary levels were replaced by "fill" and "floor fill" layers, defined by the elevation above the first floor in any room. Arbitrary levels in Room 1 were later converted into these stratigraphic units.

Following the exposure of the floor, excavators started a 5–foot (1.5-m) wide trench, running east and west directly adjacent to the south wall, to investigate cultural fill below the floor. Feature 1 and Pit House 1 were discovered in this trench, and the trench was discontinued. Feature 2 was defined later, after the floor of Room 1 had stood exposed for a brief time. After the definition of Pit House 1 but prior to the discovery of its true nature, the arbitrary levels of Room 1 were continued down into the pit house fill. These were later redesignated as fill and floor fill of Pit House 1, to correspond with the excavation units in Pit House 1 below Room 4.

Fill (Levels 1 and 2): Fill material was about 1 foot (30 cm) deep along the east wall but petered out in the northwest corner. Fill consisted of a hard, compacted, dry gray sandy soil with numerous small adobe fragments that increased in frequency with increasing depth. Few rocks of any size appeared in the fill, and the only two or three rocks present that were similar to those

observed in the cimiento foundations were located along the most eroded sections of the west wall.

Floor Fill (Level 3): Identical to Fill; limited to the 4 inches (10 cm) of material above the floor.

Floor: The floor consisted of a thin gray mud plaster applied directly over undisturbed soil, except in the south half of the room. The floor was best preserved along the east wall and was mostly eroded in the west half of the room. The floor extended over Feature 1 and Pit House 1; Feature 2 was associated with this floor.

Feature 1: Probably a posthole; pit about 12 inches in diameter and 27 inches deep (30-by-68 cm) that was defined directly below the floor surface of Room 1. The uppermost portion of the pit was lined with river cobble wedges or shims.

The floor of Room 1 extended over Feature 1, which was located just outside the east wall of Pit House 1. Excavators assumed that this pit was associated with Pit House 1; however the placement of this feature, at an identical distance from the east wall of Room 1 as Feature 2, suggests that it may have been misinterpreted in the field and that it may have formed part of a structure with Feature 2, if, in fact, Feature 2 was a posthole. Feature 1 is described with Pit House 1.

Feature 2: A cylindrical pit, 8 inches in diameter and 27 inches deep (20-by-68 cm). At 20 inches (50 cm) below the floor surface, a loose adobe hemispherical plug was resting on the sterile sand filling the lower part of the pit. Above this plug, the walls of the pit were lined with a relatively thick (1 inch) smooth mud plaster. This pit is shaped like a posthole, but the convex adobe base plug and the plastered walls do not support such a function nor do they suggest any other function.

Room 2

Condition prior to excavation: Room 2 was located in the deepest portion of the mound and was the least disturbed unit in the main room block (Fig. 3.3).

Sequence of excavation: Fill was removed to 3 to 5 inches (7 to 12 cm) above Floor 1 and material recovered was designated Fill. Remaining fill above floor was removed and designated Floor Fill. The floor was cleared, and Features 3, 4, and 5 were excavated. Subsequently, Features 6 and 7 were defined and excavated. Feature 6 was the upper portion of a poorly defined pit, the lower portions of which were subsequently defined as Features 8 and 9. These last two features, and Feature 17, were probably associated with Floor 1. Floor 2, a designation used only in the field, referred to the floor of Pit House 2. Features 8, 9, and 17 were defined during the excavation of Pit House 2.

Fill: Depth from 6 to 8 inches (15 to 20 cm) across the entire room; fill similar to that in Room 1; almost no rocks of any size.

Floor Fill: 3 to 5 inches in depth; identical to fill.

Floor (Designated "Floor 1"): Well defined, thin, gray mud plaster applied directly on undisturbed soil, except over Pit House 2. All features defined in this room appear to be associated with this floor. Two manos were on the floor: GS 4 just south of the firepit (Feature 3) and GS 5 (Fig. B.5*e, f*) at the base of the west wall, almost exactly at its midpoint. A partial plain brown ware bowl (Feature 5) was just below and near the center of the east wall.

Feature 3: A square slab-lined and slab-floored firepit, about 20–by–18–by–8 inches deep (50–by–45–by–20 cm), set 6 inches (15 cm) below floor level with slabs projecting about 2 inches (5 cm) above the floor. The firepit had been constructed prior to laying the floor plaster, presumably in a single construction episode. The pit was filled with light gray ashy sand to 2 inches below the floor surface. Two fragments of a slab metate (GS 6; Fig. B.5*p*) had been used in lining the pit.

Feature 4: Poorly defined pit, about 10 inches (25 cm) in diameter at floor level and narrowing to about 4 inches (10 cm) in diameter at the pit's base, which was about 9 inches (23 cm) below floor level. Fill was identical to room fill. No evidence of function; possibly a posthole.

Feature 5: A partial brown ware smudged-polished-interior bowl, on the floor just below and near the center of the east wall.

Features 6, 8, and 9. Feature 6 was a rock-filled pit, sealed at floor level, but with half a dozen large river cobbles projecting slightly above floor level. Below the definable pit in the floor surface, pit outlines could not be defined in the fill of Pit House 2; however, the concentration of river cobbles continued below Feature 6 and was designated Feature 8. Below Feature 8, in a shallow, clearly defined pit through the floor of Pit House 2, was Feature 9, a poorly preserved inhumation, accompanied by a large sherd of a small indented corrugated jar.

Features 6, 8, and 9 represent an oval pit, running roughly north-south in the northeast corner of Room 2, with dimensions at the floor level of about 36–by–27 inches (91–by–68 cm), with a slight extension to the southwest. At its base, about 24 inches (61 cm) below Floor 1 of Room 2 and extending 8 inches to 10 inches (20 to 25 cm) below the floor of Pit House 2, the pit

measured 43 inches north-south by 20 inches east-west (1.1–by–0.5 m). The base of the pit was fairly flat. The pit extended 2 inches to 4 inches (5 to 10 cm) beneath the east wall of Room 2 at its south end. An adult of more than 18 years and of unknown gender had been placed in the south half of the pit, with the head to the south and the knees up, body flexed. The burial, as preserved, extended 2 inches above the level of the floor of Pit House 2 and in this portion above the body the pit was packed with river cobbles (in the south half of the pit), with a partial small indented corrugated jar in the north end of the pit just above the level of the pit house floor. The entire pit opening was filled with river cobbles at the floor level of Room 2, with the space between the cobbles filled with an adobe similar to that used in floor construction. Pottery recovered from pit fill included 3 sherds of plain brown ware, 7 sherds of clapboard corrugated, 1 sherd of Chupadero Black-on-white, and 1 sherd of Tularosa Fillet-rim.

Feature 7: Feature 7 was an unlined, basin-shaped pit measuring 12 inches to 13 inches in diameter and 8.5 inches deep (about 32–by–21 cm) below floor surface. The pit was partially filled with ashy sand, with a large fragmented plain brown ware sherd in the bottom of the pit. The pit appeared to be unfired.

Feature 17: Probably a posthole located 6 inches east of the slab-lined firepit (Feature 3). It was defined during the excavation of Pit House 2, but was located just below the floor surface of Room 2. Cobble wedges lined the east, south, and west sides of the 6–inch (15–cm) diameter pit. No well-defined base for this feature could be located, but the pit was at least 12 inches in depth, and probably deeper.

Room 3

Condition prior to excavation: The east wall and the northeast corner of the room were badly eroded. The southeast corner had been disturbed by a recent pothole, designated Feature 14. Four small mesquite bushes were growing in the north and south ends of the room.

Sequence of excavation: Fill was removed to 4 inches (10 cm) above the floor, where it could be defined, and to an equivalent depth in areas where the floor was poorly defined. Floor Fill, the remaining fill above floor, was removed exposing the floor. Feature 14 was excavated, and subfloor tests were made in all areas of the room. Pit House 2, which underlay the northwest corner of the room, was excavated.

Fill: Depth diminished from 6 inches (15 cm) along the west wall to surface at the east wall, which was eroded below floor level. Fill was identical to that of Room 1. There were almost no rocks of any size, even in the deeper east portion of the room.

Floor Fill: 4 inches (10 cm) in depth in the west half of the room, pinching out about two-thirds of the way across the room. Identical to Fill.

Floor: Not well defined in any portion of the room, but nonexistent in the eastern one-third. Appeared to be an irregular surface on undisturbed soil, except over Pit House 2, where it was difficult to define. Probably not plastered. No features associated with this floor.

Feature 14. Recent pothole or disturbance to a depth of about 2.5 feet (74 cm) below the floor level.

Room 4

Conditions prior to excavation: Room 4, like Room 1, was eroded somewhat to the west. A shallow disturbance, probably an aborted pothole, was located in the southwest corner of the room. It did not extend far below the probable floor level (which could not be defined in the west portion of the room). A large yucca was growing next to the west wall, near the midpoint.

Sequence of excavation: Fill was removed to within 4 inches (10 cm) of the floor, with recovered materials labeled as Fill. Remaining fill was removed and designated Floor Fill. The floor was cleared, and Features 10 and 11 were excavated. Subfloor tests were made. The Room 4 floor over Pit House 2 had settled almost an inch, clearly defining this structure prior to subfloor excavations.

Fill: Depth varied from about 12 inches (30 cm) along the east wall to less than 2 inches (5 cm) along the west wall. Fill similar to that in Room 1. Almost no rocks of sufficient size to be considered as wall rubble were encountered in the fill.

Floor Fill: 3 to 4 inches (7 to 10 cm) deep across entire room; identical to fill.

Floor: Well preserved along the east wall where the room was excavated into the mesa top to a depth of 8 inches (20 cm). The floor was flanged or coped onto the wall face, which was also plastered. Both wall and floor plaster were very smooth, almost polished, gray clay about 1 inch thick (about twice as thick as floor plastering in other rooms) applied directly on undisturbed soil. This floor was relatively well preserved in the center portion of the room, but was eroded and patchy in the west third of the room. Features 10 and 11 were associated with this floor.

Feature 10. A rectangular, partially slab-lined and slab-floored firepit. The firepit was 23-by-17-by-8

inches (58-by-43-by-20 cm) deep, with approximately 2 inches (5 cm) of the slabs extending above the floor level. The north side of the pit was only partially lined, and the floor of the pit was lined only with one small cobble in the southwest corner. The pit was excavated into the fill of Pit House 2, and the north wall and base of the pit were indistinct and poorly defined. Fill was similar to room fill.

Feature 11. Pit, almost identical to Feature 2 in Room 1. The pit was about 10 inches in diameter and 26 inches deep (25-by-66 cm). It was adobe lined to a depth of about 18 inches (45 cm) below floor level; a loose hemispherical adobe plug rested in the sterile sand fill of the pit at this level.

Room 5

Condition prior to excavation: Room 5, like Room 2, was in the deepest portion of the mound, and was well preserved.

Sequence of excavation: Fill removed to 4 inches (10 cm) above floor; material designated Fill. Remaining fill removed to floor and designated Floor Fill. Floor cleared, Feature 12B excavated, and subfloor tests placed across entire area of room.

Fill: Depth from 6 to 8 inches (15 to 20 cm) across entire room; fill similar to that in Room 1. Almost no rocks of sizes suitable for wall masonry in the fill.

Floor Fill: 4 inches (10 cm) in depth; identical to Fill.

Floor: Well defined across entire room. Thin gray mud plaster applied directly on undisturbed soil. Feature 12B associated with this floor. Some wall plaster, over wall stubs, was noted along the north section of the east wall. Floor plaster flanged onto wall plaster. A pestle (GS 8; Fig. B.5*k*) was on the floor at approximately the center of the southwest quadrant.

Wall features: About midway along the east wall, there were no wall foundation stones or wall stubs for a distance of about 2.5 feet (74 cm). This gap did not appear to represent a disturbance and perhaps indicated a doorway.

Feature 12B. Unlined, rectangular firepit measuring 18-by-15-by-5 inches deep (46-by-38-by-13 cm). The firepit was filled to floor level with gray ashy sand.

Pit House 1

Condition prior to excavation: Pit House 1 was located beneath Rooms 1 and 4. The portion of Pit House 1 outside of the room block was not excavated.

Sequence of excavation: Pit House 1 was originally discovered in an exploratory trench along the south wall of Room 1. This trench destroyed much of the wall structure of the pit house below Room 1. Fill of the pit house was removed in the arbitrary 6–inch levels used in Room 1. The floor of Room 4 had sunk slightly to reveal the outlines of the pit house in this area, and the excavation of the structure proceeded in a less destructive manner. Fill below Room 4 was removed in two layers, Fill and Floor Fill. The floor of the structure was cleared and Features 12A and 13 were excavated.

Fill (Level 4 in Room 1): Dark brown loose sand, with frequent charcoal fragments, ranging to burned beams up to 3 inches (8 cm) in diameter in the fill below Room 4. These beams were too fragmentary for dendrochronological dating, but one sample on an unknown wood (possibly pine) produced a ^{14}C date of BP 980 ± 80 (N–1588). The frequent large pieces of burned adobe presumably were roof fragments, but no beam impressions were noted. Along the south wall of the pit house, the fill contained numerous, small river cobbles that did not appear to have been burned. The fill layer was approximately 6 inches (15 cm) in depth and was equivalent to Level 5 in Room 1.

Floor Fill: Identical to Fill; varied from 4 inches to 6 inches deep (10 to 15 cm).

Floor: Floor and wall plaster was burned and well preserved, particularly in the southern half of the pit house, below Room 4. The floor and wall plaster was less than one-half inch thick and was applied directly on undisturbed soil. The plaster was gray and well smoothed. Wall plaster appeared to have been truncated at floor level in Room 4; this juncture was destroyed in Room 1. Features 12A and 13 were associated with this floor.

Feature 1. Feature 1 was excavated with Room 1 (see above), but it is likely that this feature, a stone-wedge-lined posthole, was actually associated with Pit House 1. It was located just outside the east wall of the pit house, at about the middle of that wall, and may have been a part of the roof support system or wall of Pit House 1.

Feature 12A. Similar to Features 2 and 11, this pit was an adobe-lined cylindrical pit about 5 inches in diameter and 17 inches deep (13–by–43 cm) below the pit house floor. The floor plaster was carried over to line the pit. There was no well-defined base. Fill was identical to pit house fill.

Feature 13. Feature 13 was a symmetrical adobe-lined, basin-shaped firepit. It measured 9 inches in diameter and 6 inches deep (23–by–15 cm). The lower one-third was filled with ashy sand, and the upper two-thirds contained room fill (see above).

Pit House 2

Condition prior to excavation: Pit House 2 (Fig. 3.4) was located beneath Rooms 2 and 3. The portion outside the room block was not excavated.

Sequence of excavation: Fill in the pit house was removed to within 4 inches (10 cm) of the floor, and recovered material was designated as Fill. The remaining material was removed as Floor Fill. The floor was cleared and Feature 16 was excavated. The fill of Pit House 2 below Room 2 was greatly disturbed by intrusive pits (Features 4, 6, 7, 8, 9, and 17).

Fill: Dark brown loose sand, with frequent charcoal and burned adobe fragments. Density of charcoal and burned adobe was somewhat less than that in the fill of Pit House 1. A small fragmented basin-shaped firepit in the fill near the west wall of the pit house was in a burned adobe mass identical to the other fragments in the fill; it was designated as Feature 15. Fragmentary vessels of a patterned indented corrugated jar and a Three Rivers Red-on-terracotta bowl were also in the fill, in uncertain association with Feature 15. In the east third of the excavated portion of the pit house, the fill contained numerous unburned river cobbles. Fill was about 8 inches deep (20 cm) below Room 2 and up to 16 inches deep (41 cm) below Room 3.

Floor Fill: 4 inches (10 cm) deep across entire floor, except where cut by Feature 9; identical to Fill.

Floor: Burned and well defined, similar to the floor of Pit House 1, consisting of a thin, smooth, gray plaster (less than 1 inch thick) applied directly on undisturbed soil. The plaster did not extend up the walls, which consequently were not as well defined as those of Pit House 1. Feature 16 was associated with this floor. A single large brown ware jar sherd was on the floor.

Feature 15. Fragmented adobe basin-shaped firepit, floating in the fill of Pit House 2 below Room 3. The firepit was at least 8 inches in diameter and at least 3 inches deep (about 20–by–8 cm).

Feature 16. Feature 16 was a slab-lined firepit in the floor of Pit House 2. The firepit measured 11–by–12–by–6 inches deep (28–by–30–by–15 cm), with the slabs projecting 1 inch to 2 inches above the floor level. The firepit had been constructed at the time the floor plaster was applied. The walls of the pit were square, with a single slab forming each wall, but the base of the pit, which was adobe lined, was basin-shaped. Fill of the firepit was identical to the fill of the pit house.

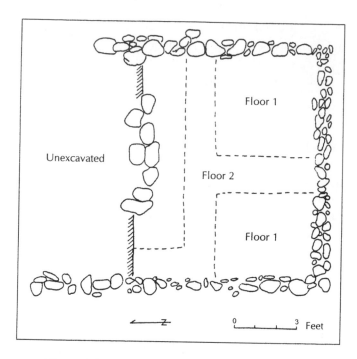

Figure 3.5. Plan of Unit A; Floor 2 was exposed only in the narrow trenches, as indicated.

Unit A

Unit A (designated as "B" in Lekson and Klinger 1973) was an isolated masonry room approximately 100 feet (30.5 m) southwest of the main room block (Figs. 3.1, 3.5). The west, south, and east walls were well defined, but the north edge of the excavation was bounded by an incomplete cross wall. The north exterior wall of the unit was not excavated. Walls consisted of stubs of river cobbles, one or two rocks in height and up to three rocks in width, set horizontally (unlike the vertical rock foundations of the main room block). These walls rested on sterile substrate, with no foundations.

Conditions prior to excavation: Unit A appeared to be a low mound of rather large river cobbles. No walls were visible originally.

Sequence of excavation: Initial trenching exposed the south wall, and subsequent shallow trenching defined the east and west walls and possibly a northern cross wall. A 5–by–5–foot (1.5–by–1.5 m) unit was excavated to Floor 1 in the southeast corner of the room; the fill of this unit was screened to approximately 3 inches (8 cm) above Floor 1 and removed as Floor Fill. In the remainder of the unit, fill above Floor Fill was removed without screening. The Floor Fill above Floor 1 was removed and screened and Floor 1 was exposed; there were no features associated with it. North-south and east-west trenches, intersecting in a T, were excavated below Floor 1 to Floor 2. These trenches were approximately 1.5 feet (46 cm) wide. Floor 2 was about 10 inches below Floor 1; Fill 2 and Floor Fill 2 were removed and screened, and the floor exposed. Tests below Floor 2 showed that this floor was located directly on undisturbed soil. Floor 2 was not cleared outside the north-south and east-west trenches, with the exception of one short extension of these trenches along the west wall.

Fill 1: Fill 1 (above the Floor Fill of Floor 1) was screened only in the 5-by-5-foot square test. The fill contained numerous river cobbles and some adobe fragments interpreted as roofing materials. Fill was between 4 inches and 8 inches (10 to 20 cm) deep.

Floor Fill 1: 2–3 inches (5 to 7 cm) of fill directly above Floor 1; identical to Fill 1.

Floor 1: A well-defined clay plaster floor, articulating with the south, west, and east walls. The relationship of this floor to the north cross wall was unclear. No features were associated with this floor.

Fill 2: Similar to Fill 1, but lacking the rubble and adobe materials of the upper fill.

Floor Fill 2: Identical to Fill 2.

Floor 2: A well-defined thin clay plaster applied directly on undisturbed soil; no associated features.

Unit B

Unit B (designated "D" in Lekson and Klinger 1973) was a surface concentration of river cobbles, forming a round or circular "pavement." It was about 10 feet (3 m) in diameter and located about 80 feet (24 m) northeast of the main block of rooms (Figs. 3.1, 3.6). This feature resembles circular stone pavements found in plaza areas at Swarts Ruin (Cosgrove and Cosgrove 1932, Plate 15b); they may have been the base levels of granaries, such as those found in Salado sites in the Tonto Basin or in cliff-sheltered sites in Chihuahua.

Condition prior to excavation: Unit B was a low mound of river cobbles, with no outlines of walls or indication of structure. Rock density was higher in the south half of the circular cluster than in the north half.

Sequence of excavation: A 5-by-5-foot (1.5–by–1.5 m) test was placed in the middle of the unit. After clearing the surface rock, a single 6 inch (15 cm) level was excavated. Undisturbed soil was encountered less than 2 inches below the ground surface and the test was discontinued.

Fill: Two inches of loose sandy surface soil, with a few surface artifacts, and below that, undisturbed soil.

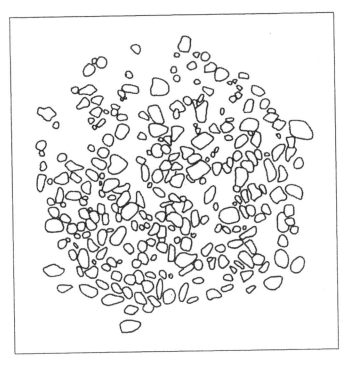

Figure 3.6. Plan of Unit B, a circular river cobble "pavement," approximately 3 meters in diameter.

Unit C

Unit C ("C" in Lekson and Klinger 1973) was a surface concentration of river cobbles about 110 feet (33.5 m) north of the main room block. The outline of Unit C was subrectangular, measuring about 8-by-10 feet (2-by-3 m). No tests were made in this unit, which was probably an isolated room.

Test Pit 1

Test Pit 1 was located about 30 feet (9 m) north of the main room block (Fig. 3.1), in a suspected trash area between the main room block and Units B and C.

Conditions prior to excavation: The surface of the ground appeared no different than that of the ground surface to the east, south, and west of the main room block; however, artifact density was notably much higher than elsewhere in the area.

Sequence of excavation: A 5-by-5 foot (1.5-by-1.5 m) test was excavated in two arbitrary 6-inch (15-cm) levels. Cultural material was only in the top 3 inches (7.6 cm). The entire second level was in undisturbed soil, and the test was discontinued.

Fill: Upper 3 inches (7.6 cm) were a brownish sand with frequent artifacts, but no constructional debris. The

lower 3 inches of Level 1, and all of Level 2, were in undisturbed natural sediments.

Other Features

Water Control Features

Two features that may have functioned as check dams were located 70 feet and 110 feet (21 m, 33.5 m) east of the site, across the upper slopes of a minor ravine (Fig. 3.1). Both were roughly piled crescents of rounded cobbles. One was 8 feet wide and about 30 feet long (2.4-by-9.1 m), and the other was about 4 feet wide and 10 feet long (1-by-3 m).

Isolated Room

An unexcavated cobble feature presumed to be an isolated room, measuring approximately 10-by-7 feet (3-by-2 m), was located on a finger of the bench on which Villareal II was located, approximately 250 feet (76 m) northwest of the main room block.

SURFACE COLLECTIONS

An extensive surface scatter of lithics and ceramics covered the bench surface, from the downslope forward edge (where the room block was located) back to the lower slopes of the valley walls (along the line of New Mexico State Route 211). The scatter extended across an area in excess of 6.25 acres (2.5 hectares) and probably represented something more than the activities of the inhabitants of the main room block. An intensive search of the bench surface disclosed no architectural features beyond those just described. A program of controlled surface collections was undertaken as an initial step toward understanding the large artifact scatter.

A series of regularly spaced 10-by-10 feet (3-by-3 m) square collection units were projected over the surface of the bench and total collections were made within each unit (Fig. 3.7). The collection units were spaced at 20-foot (6 m) intervals around the main room block and at 50-foot (15 m) intervals across the major portion of the bench. In the 180-by-260 foot (55-by-79 m) area around the main room block, the collection units represented a 7 percent sample of the bench surface. When this area is corrected for the presence of the excavated structures and steeply sloping forward edges of the bench, the area sample approaches 10 percent. Over the remainder of the bench, the collection units covered about 3 percent of the bench surface; combined, about

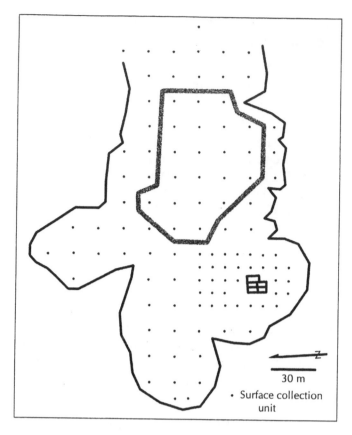

Figure 3.7. Distribution of surface collection units. The aceramic lithic surface concentration was located within the gray outline.

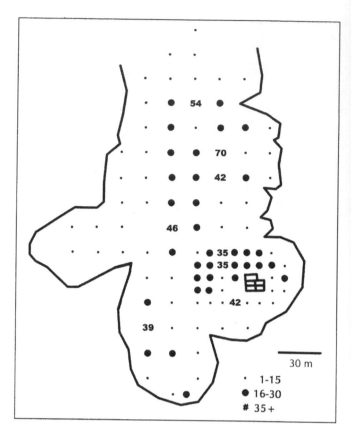

Figure 3.8. Density of flakes in surface collection units.

4 percent of the bench surface was sampled. I made these collections during a two-day period in 1973 with a crew of two, whose names, unfortunately, I cannot remember. The material was designated "VT" and, like the names of the suffering crew, the significance of the "T" portion of this designation is lost and past recovery except, perhaps, by a hypnotist. The "V" presumably stood for Villareal. But, the "T"?

Materials recovered from the systematic surface collections totaled 1,617 chipped stone artifacts, 494 sherds, and no ground stone. Some ground stone pieces had been previously collected from the area immediately around the main room block during excavation of that structure.

Figures 3.8 through 3.11 show the distribution of flakes, tools and cores, decorated ceramics, and undecorated ceramics. Timothy Klinger classified the ceramics in the surface collections, and I analyzed the lithics using a modified form of a typology developed by James Fitting (1972b) and Roger Moore (Appendix B). Unmodified debitage and utilized flakes were not separated into flake types and were simply classified

as "flakes." Instead of eight classes of materials, only three were used: Coarse (including basalt, andesite, rhyolite, and quartzite), Fine (including chert, chalcedony, and agate), and Obsidian.

There were at least two areas of high lithic artifact density (defined as units with more than 20 artifacts). One was around the room block; the other ("northeast" concentration) was approximately 125 feet (38 m) northeast of the main room block and measured about 300 feet east-west by 200 feet north-south (91-by-61 m; Fig. 3.8). The boundary between the two concentrations was not discrete, but nevertheless fairly clear.

Collection units with the highest density of cores occurred in the "northeast" lithic concentration, and most of the remaining cores were in the room block concentration (Fig. 3.9). However, no finished tools appeared within the boundaries of the "northeast" concentration. Most finished tools, which were almost exclusively projectile points and bifacial perforators, were located around the room block, with the remainder either near the unexcavated isolated room northwest of the main room block or in an isolated cluster north of the "northeast" lithic concentration.

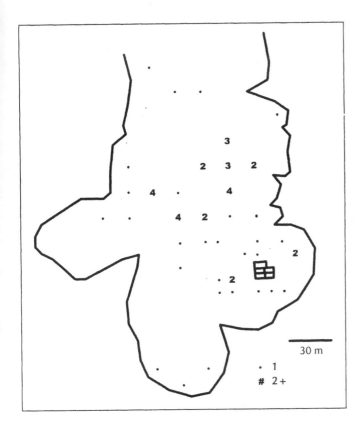

Figure 3.9. Density of lithic tools and
cores in surface collection units.

Figure 3.10. Density of plain ware
sherds in surface collection units.

The ceramics were strongly clustered in an oval area about 400 feet north-south by 250 feet east-west (122-by-76 m) around the main room block. This area contained about 80 percent of the sherds, but only 35 percent of the lithic pieces. Collection unit density was more than twice as great in this area than across the remainder of the bench surface, but even if only those collection units falling in the 50-foot (15-m) grid spacing were considered, the ceramic concentration around the room block was still clearly evident. Decorated ceramics were especially concentrated around the room block; only four decorated sherds were recovered along the north edge and the westernmost extension of the bench, all undifferentiated white wares presumably of the Mimbres series. Ceramic materials were more densely concentrated to the north and east of the room block. Lithic materials were dense to the north and east of the room block, but also heavily concentrated just to the west of the structure.

The ground surface slopes fairly steeply away from the room block to the west (see Fig. 3.1). There is a gentler slope to the east, toward the gully with the two check dams. The fact that the heaviest concentrations of

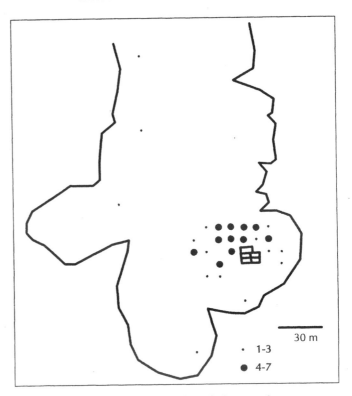

Figure 3.11. Density of decorated
sherds in surface collection units.

lithics and ceramics occurred to the east of the room block may be related to these differences in slope. The east slope is almost completely eroded to the Gila conglomerate, with topsoil removed through sheet erosion toward the check dams below. Artifacts in this area, which may have been the main trash dump for the room block, may be erosional residuals, since the cultural deposit has no depth; that is, the artifacts may be naturally concentrated through the erosion of finer grained sediments and soils. High artifact concentrations in the far less eroded and level areas north of the room block indicate that midden deposits might have existed there, but test excavations (Test Pit 1, above) disclosed that those deposits were less than 3 inches deep.

CONTEXTS AND ASSOCIATIONS

The basic stratigraphy of Villareal II was simple: a room block with five rooms was built over two semi-subterranean pit houses (Fig. 3.4). Wall trenches for seating cimientos and various floor features intruded into the fill of the two pit houses, but plastered floors sealed over the lower pit house fill. It is not clear if the pit houses were filled prior to or during construction of the room block. Dates for the ceramics in the fill of Pit House 1 indicate filling occurred significantly prior to room block construction, whereas ceramics recovered in the fill of Pit House 2 contained more late types that indicate either filling at the time of pueblo construction or a high level of disturbance (such as a burial pit intruding into and through the floor of Pit House 2 from Room 2 of the room block).

The shallow depth of fill over much of the room block made the separation of fill and floor fill difficult and sometimes impossible. Thus a basic context used in this report is the "architectural unit": the fill, floor fill, floor, and associated features within a single room or a single pit house. Some analyses, as indicated below, also use divisions between "fill" and "floor fill–floor" within architectural units.

Contexts within rooms are defined in individual unit descriptions. Perhaps the most complex context is the association of Features 6, 8, and 9. Together, they denote a burial pit and inhumation associated with the floor of Room 2 that intruded through the fill and floor of Pit House 2. In the field, the inhumation was originally considered to be associated with Pit House 2, but subsequent work clarified its association with the later Room 2.

CERAMICS

Stephen H. Lekson and Timothy C. Klinger

Timothy Klinger analyzed the ceramics using the Upper Gila Project typology (Klinger 1975). Collections from excavations totaled about 4,900 sherds; there were no restorable vessels. Counts of sherds by contexts are in Table 3.1.

In both rooms and pit houses at Villareal II, decorated sherds accounted for only 8 to 13 percent of the total sherds and nondecorated sherds ranged from 87 to 92 percent of the total ceramics from each architectural unit. Alma series types were the most common, contributing 57 to 67 percent, except in Pit House 2 where Alma series types were only 45 percent of all sherds, and in Unit A where Alma series pottery made up only 28 percent of all sherds. San Francisco Red pottery was present in minor amounts (2.0-7.5%) in all architectural units. Clapboard Corrugated ranged from 15 to 20 percent in room contexts. In Pit House 1, this type made up only 10 percent of the collections, but in Pit House 2 and Unit A it was notably more abundant (37% and 50% respectively). Indented corrugated was present in minor amounts (less than 3%) in room and pit house contexts (except Room 5), as were red-slipped incised and cord-marked ceramics.

Mimbres Classic Black-on-white was by far the most abundant decorated pottery, between 1.8 and 6 percent in all rooms and pit houses at Villareal II except Unit A, where it was entirely absent. Mimbres Boldface Black-on-white was present in very small amounts in all units except Rooms 4 and 5. Three sherds of Boldface Black-on-white were in the collections from Unit A (where no Mimbres Classic Black-on-white appeared). Chupadero Black-on-white was present in small amounts in all rooms and pit houses. Other black-on-white types included Socorro Black-on-white (found only in Room 1) and Tularosa Black-on-white (recorded only in Pit Houses 1 and 2). Wingate Black-on-red was present in the rooms (except Room 2) and in Pit House 1 at Villareal II, but absent elsewhere. St. Johns Polychrome was limited to a single surface sherd in the vicinity of the room block. Gila Polychrome was present in small quantities in all rooms and in Pit House 2, but was well represented only in Room 5. Gila Polychrome was accompanied by small amounts of Tonto Polychrome and Tucson Polychrome in Room 3, by Tonto Polychrome only in Room 2, and by Tucson Polychrome only in Room 5. El Paso Polychrome occurred only in Room 3 and in Pit House 2.

Table 3.1. Ceramics from Excavations at Villareal II

Ceramics	Room 1 Fill	Floor Fill	Floor	Feature 1	Room 2 Fill	Floor Fill	Floor	Feat. 3	Feat. 4 & 7	Feature 9
Alma Series	135	133	42	1	379	204	4	2	19	3
San Francisco Series	9	8	1	3	22	24	2	1		
Clapboard corrugated	56	35	7		111	37	2			7
Neck banded										
Indented corrugated	3	1				1				
Incised	5	7			15	3				
Playas Red Incised	2				2					
Indented	5	1			11	2				
Indented-incised										
Cord-marked	1	1	1		7	2				
Cord-marked-incised										
Tularosa Fillet-rim					3					
Gila Red					3	5	1			
Gila Corrugated										
Mimbres Boldface B/W		1			1					
Mimbres Classic B/W	11	7	1		23	9				
Tularosa Black-on-white										
Chupadero Black-on-white		4			5	1				
Socorro Black-on-white	1									
Undifferentiated B/W										
Undifferentiated white ware	14	5			35	4	1			
Wingate Black-on-red	2		1							
Unknown black-on-red						1				
St. Johns Polychrome										
Gila Polychrome		4			2	1				
Tonto Polychrome					1		3			
Tucson Polychrome										
El Paso Polychrome										
Unknown		1	1		10	3				
Total	244	208	54	4	630	297	13	3	19	10

Ceramics	Room 3 Fill	Floor Fill	Floor	Room 4 Fill	Floor Fill	Floor	Feat. 10	Room 5 Fill	Floor Fill	Floor
Alma Series	450	240	64	138	90	4	5	266	69	1
San Francisco Series	10	13	4	13	16	2		17	4	
Clapborad corrugated	120	35	12	39	29	1	1	79	19	1
Neck banded	6		2							
Indented corrugated	1	5	2	6	2					
Incised	13	5		2	1			8	4	
Playas Red Incised	4		1	2	3			6		
Indented	10	4	4	4	7					
Indented-incised			1							
Cord-marked		1		1	1			2	3	
Cord-marked-incised										
Tularosa Fillet-rim										
Gila Red	5	12	3							
Gila Corrugated										
Mimbres Boldface B/W	1									
Mimbres Classic B/W	15	6		5	7			18	1	
Tularosa Black-on-white										
Chupadero Black-on-white	7			3	1			2		
Socorro Black-on-white										
Undifferentiated B/W										
Undifferentiated white ware	23	8	1	11	6			13	2	
Wingate Black-on-red	5			1				2		
Unknown black-on-red										
St. Johns Polychrome										
Gila Polychrome	5	2			1			12	3	4
Tonto Polychrome	2		1							
Tucson Polychrome	2							1		1
El Paso Polychrome	3	1	1					1		
Unknown				5	4					
Total	682	332	96	230	168	7	6	427	105	7

Table 3.1. Ceramics from Excavations at Villareal II (continued)

Ceramics	Room 5 Feat. 12B	Pit House 1 Fill	Floor Fill	Floor	Pit House 2 Fill	Floor Fill	Floor	Feat. 14	Unit A Fill 1	Floor Fill 1
Alma Series	3	253	38	9	200	53	7	16	25	3
San Francisco Series		22	4		6	7		2	4	1
Clapborad corrugated		44	7	3	147	52	13	11	38	15
Neck banded										
Indented corrugated		3			4				3	
Incised		13	1	1	2					
Playas Red Incised		10		2	1					
Indented		10	2	1	1					1
Indented-incised										
Cord-marked		1	1					1		
Cord-marked-incised					1					
Tularosa Fillet-rim		1	1							
Gila Red										
Gila Corrugated										
Mimbres Boldface B/W		2						2	1	1
Mimbres Classic B/W		11	3	1	20	12	4			
Tularosa Black-on-white		9			2					
Chupadero Black-on-white		5		3	2				3	
Socorro Black-on-white										
Undifferentiated B/W										
Undifferentiated white ware		13			19	7	4		5	2
Wingate Black-on-red		2								
Unknown black-on-red										
St. Johns Polychrome										
Gila Polychrome						1				
Tonto Polychrome										
Tucson Polychrome										
El Paso Polychrome					4			1		
Unknown		10	1	1	2				1	
Total	3	409	58	21	411	132	30	31	80	23

Ceramics	Unit A Floor 1	Fill 2	Floor 2	Unit B	Test Pit 1 Level 1
Alma Series		3	5	3	70
San Francisco Series		1			
Clapborad corrugated	4	5	2		13
Neck banded					
Indented corrugated		1			1
Incised					
Playas Red Incised					
Indented		1	1		
Indented-incised					
Cord-marked					
Cord-marked-incised					
Tularosa Fillet-rim					
Gila Red					
Gila Corrugated					
Mimbres Boldface B/W			1		
Mimbres Classic B/W					
Tularosa Black-on-white					
Chupadero Black-on-white				1	
Socorro Black-on-white					
Undifferentiated B/W					
Undifferentiated white ware		1			
Wingate Black-on-red					
Unknown black-on-red					
St. Johns Polychrome					
Gila Polychrome					
Tonto Polychrome					
Tucson Polychrome					
El Paso Polychrome					
Unknown					
Total	4	11	10	4	84

The "architectural unit" ceramic assemblages of Rooms 1 through 5 can be characterized as 55 to 65 percent Alma series, 2.5 to 7.5 percent San Francisco series, 15 to 20 percent clapboard corrugated, with traces of indented corrugated, incised, and cord-marked pottery. Decorated ceramics typically contributed about 2 to 4 percent Mimbres Classic Black-on-white, with small quantities of Mimbres Boldface Black-on-white, Chupadero Black-on-white, Wingate Black-on-red, and Gila Polychrome. Socorro Black-on-white, Tularosa Black-on-white, Tonto Polychrome, Tucson Polychrome, and El Paso Polychrome were represented by one or two sherds in a few rooms.

The ceramic assemblages from pit house "architectural units" were more varied. The Pit House 1 pottery resembled assemblages from the pueblo rooms, but lacked Gila Polychrome. Pit House 2 differed from both rooms and Pit House 1, with lower frequencies of the

Alma series (45%), higher frequencies of clapboard corrugated (37%), and higher frequencies of Mimbres Black-on-white (almost 6%). One sherd of Gila Polychrome was found in the fill of Pit House 2.

Brainerd-Robinson indices were calculated for room and pit house fill and for combined floor-fill and floor assemblages. The Brainerd-Robinson matrix suggested that fill deposits in Rooms 1, 2, and 3 were more alike than those in Rooms 4 and 5, which differed slightly from all other rooms. The fills of Pit Houses 1 and 2 were not alike. The Brainerd-Robinson matrix of combined floor-fill and floor suggested that Rooms 1, 2, 3, and 4 were fairly similar, but Room 5 was distinctive. The floor-fill and floors of Pit Houses 1 and 2 differed from each other. Several points emerged from this analysis: the floor–fill and floor assemblage in Room 5 was relatively unlike the other surface rooms; the two pit houses differed from each other in both fill and floor-fill plus floor assemblages; and the Unit A assemblage was unique. Room 5 had more than 80 percent of the Gila Polychrome at the site, from fill, floor-fill, and floor contexts. Compared with Pit House 1, Pit House 2 had relatively low proportions of plain wares and relatively high proportions of clapboard corrugated and Mimbres Classic Black-on-white. The distinctive ceramic assemblage of Unit A contained low percentages of Alma series pottery, high percentages of clapboard and indented corrugated, an absence of incised and cord-marked, high frequencies of Mimbres Boldface, but no Mimbres Classic Black-on-white and no Salado polychromes.

NONCERAMIC MATERIALS

The limited information available on flaked and ground stone artifacts, recorded in 1972, is presented in Appendix B. Site contexts for the tools are briefly summarized in Table 3.2.

The "northeast" surface concentration was distinct from the room block and pit house lithic assemblages. The surface collection included earlier projectile point forms and higher proportions of coarse materials and obsidian than the room block and pit houses.

Two shell ornaments were in the fill of Room 5. One was a "figure 8" bead of unknown species and the second was a small fragment of a shell bracelet, probably *Glycymeris* sp.

The few fragmentary bone artifacts included a tubular bead fragment of an unknown small-medium mammal long bone shaft (Room 3, floor); a worked fragment of an unknown medium-large mammal long bone

Table 3.2. Flaked and Ground Stone Artifacts at Villareal II

Room 1: 456 flakes, 2 cores, 10 tools.
   Cores, choppers and chopping tools, and combination tools were concentrated in this room. A unifacial perforator was found on the floor.
Room 2: 385 flakes, 3 cores, 7 tools.
   Plano-convex cores appeared to be concentrated in the fill and floor fill of Room 2.
Room 3: 192 flakes, 2 cores, 4 tools.
   Room 3 was remarkable for its raw materials and flakes. It had the lowest percentage of chert and the highest percentages of basalt and rhyolite of any room. It also had the highest proportion of blocky flakes. These two trends are intriguing because basalt and rhyolite comprise a disproportionate number of flat, rather than blocky, flakes.
Room 4: 311 flakes, 2 cores, 5 tools.
   A projectile point was on the floor.
Room 5: 260 flakes, 5 tools.
Pit House 1: 104 flakes, 1 core, 4 tools.
   Pit House 1 had an unusually high proportion of basalt.
Pit House 2: 134 flakes, 3 cores, 3 tools.

shaft (Pit House 2 fill); an awl or needle from the proximal shaft fragment of a *Sylvilagus* left tibia, the distal end of which had been ground (Pit House 2, floor fill); an awl made from the proximal anterior crest of an artiodactyl tibia, probably a deer (Pit House 2, floor fill); an awl fragment from an unknown artiodactyl long bone fragment (Feature 12B); and the pointy portion of another awl from an unknown artiodactyl long bone shaft fragment (Unit A, Floor Fill 1).

FAUNAL REMAINS

William B. Gillespie

The faunal collection included 347 bones recovered from excavations at the Villareal II site. They were examined during May of 1978 using reference material at the National Park Service Chaco Center in Albuquerque. Of this total, all but 12 specimens were of mammals or were badly weathered, unidentifiable fragments, leaving a sample total of 335 elements (Table 3.3). Approximately half of the mammalian bones were identified to either the genus or species level. Included in the non-mammalian remains were three bird bones, two fish, one amphibian, five snake vertebrae, and one unidentified amphibian or reptile. These were not identified to any lower taxonomic level.

Minimum numbers of individuals (MNI) were calculated for each architectural unit (room or pit house). Within each of these units, a minimum number for each

Table 3.3. Faunal Remains at Villareal II

Taxa	Room 1 Floor Fill	Room 1 Floor	Room 2 Fill	Room 2 Floor Fill	Room 2 Floor	Room 2 Total	Room 3 Fill	Room 3 Floor	Room 3 Floor Fill	Room 3 Total	Room 4 Fill	Room 4 Floor Fill	Room 4 Floor
Sylvilagus cf. *auduboni* (cottontail)			3			3/1		1		1/1		1	1
Lepus californicus (jackrabbit)			1			1/1					1		
Cynomys ludovicianus (prairie dog)	1		1	2		3/2	1			1/1			
Thomomys bottae (pocket gopher)												2	
cf. *Dipodomys spectabilis* (cf. kangaroo rat)				1		1/1							
Neotoma sp. (wood rat)													
cf. *Canis familiaris* (cf. domestic dog)													
Procyon lotor (raccoon)			1			1/1							
Odocoileus sp. (unknown deer)							1			1/1			
Odocoileus cf. *viginianus* (cf. white-tailed deer)			1			1/1					1	1	
cf. *Odocoileus* sp. (cf. deer)								1		1			
Antilocapra americana (pronghorn)		1		4		4/1							
cf. *A. americana* (cf. pronghorn)													
Unknown rodent-sized mammal													
Unknown small-medium mammal (rabbit-large rodent)							1			1			
Unknown medium-size mammal (cf. carnivore)			5			5							
Unknown medium-large mammal (carnivore-artiodactyl)	4		13	10	1	24	13	2		15		1	
Unknown artiodactyl			5	3		8					2		
Unknown vertebrate (mostly cf. mammal)												1	
Total (mammal + cf. mammal)	5	1	30	20	1	51/8	16	4		20/3	4	6	1

Taxa	Room 4 Feat. 10	Room 4 Total	Room 5 Fill	Room 5 Total	Prov. "A" Fill 1	Prov. "A" Fill 2	Prov. "A" Floor	Prov. "A" Total	Pit House 1 Fill	Pit House 1 Floor Fill	Pit House 1 Floor	Pit House 1 Total	Pit House 2 Fill "A"
Sylvilagus cf. *auduboni* (cottontail)		2/1	1	1/1	1	1	2	4	24	7	1	32/3	1
Lepus californicus (jackrabbit)		1/1							6	6		12/2	1
Cynomys ludovicianus (prairie dog)	1	1/1							27	9	1	37/4	2
Thomomys bottae (pocket gopher)		2/1								2		2/1	6
cf. *Dipodomys spectabilis* (cf. kangaroo rat)			2	2/2									
Neotoma sp. (wood rat)							1	1/1		1		1/1	
cf. *Canis familiaris* (cf. domestic dog)													
Procyon lotor (raccoon)													
Odocoileus sp. (unknown deer)													
Odocoileus cf. *viginianus* (cf. white-tailed deer)		2/1	3	3/1									
cf. *Odocoileus* sp. (cf. deer)													
Antilocapra americana (pronghorn)									2			2/1	
cf. *A. americana* (cf. pronghorn)									1	1		2/1	
Unknown rodent-sized mammal													
Unknown small-medium mammal (rabbit-large rodent)	3	3			1		1	2	16	4		20	1
Unknown medium-size mammal (cf. carnivore)	1	1							3			3	1
Unknown medium-large mammal (carnivore-artiodactyl)	1	2	10	10		4	5	9	8	6	1	15	2
Unknown artiodactyl		2							1	3		4	1
Unknown vertebrate (mostly cf. mammal)		1								1		1	
Total	6	17/5	16	16/4	2	5	10	17/4	88	40	3	131/3	17

NOTE: In a/b entries, a is number of elements, b is estimated MNI (minimum number of individuals) calculated by major provenience units.

Table 3.3. Faunal Remains at Villareal II (continued)

Taxa	Pit House 2 Fill "B"	Floor Fill	Floor	Total	Number of Elements	Percent	MNI Number	Percent
Sylvilagus cf. *auduboni* (cottontail)	5	8	2	16/3	60	17.9	11	22.0
Lepus californicus (jackrabbit)	1	2	1	5/1	20	6.0	6	12.0
Cynomys ludovicianus (prairie dog)	2	1		5/1	50	14.9	11	22.0
Thomomys bottae (pocket gopher)	1	1		8/2	12	3.5	5	10.0
cf. *Dipodomys spectabilis* (cf. kangaroo rat)					1	0.3	1	2.0
Neotoma sp. (wood rat)	1			2/2	4	1.2	4	8.0
cf. *Canis familiaris* (cf. domestic dog)	1			1/1	1	0.3	1	2.0
Procyon lotor (raccoon)					1	0.3	1	2.0
Odocoileus sp. (unknown deer)	1			1/1	4	1.2	3	6.0
Odocoileus cf. *viginianus* (cf. white-tailed deer)					3	0.9	1	2.0
cf. *Odocoileus* sp. (cf. deer)					2	0.6	1	2.0
Antilocapra americana (pronghorn)					7	2.1	3	6.0
cf. *A. americana* (cf. pronghorn)					2	0.6	1	2.0
Unknown rodent-sized mammal				1	1	0.3		
Unknown small-medium mammal (rabbit-large rodent)	6	1	3	11	38	11.3		
Unknown medium-size mammal (cf. carnivore)				1	10	3.0		
Unknown medium-large mammal (carnivore-artiodactyl)	4	6	5	17	92	27.5	1	2.0
Unknown artiodactyl	3	2		6	21	6.3		
Unknown vertebrate (mostly cf. mammal)	3			3	6	1.8		
Total (mammal + cf. mammal)	28	21	11	77/11	335	100.0	50	100.0

NOTE: In a/b entries, a is number of elements, b as estimated MNI (minimum number of individuals) calculated by major provenience units.

genus or species was derived using the most common skeletal element (of a given side) and supplementing this number through matching characteristics (size, epiphyseal fusion). In calculating MNIs by separate major provenience units, two basic assumptions were made. One was that there was a low probability that elements of a single individual would be located in more than one architectural unit; the second was that there was a higher probability, one which could not be ignored, that a single individual might be represented in different excavation units within each architectural unit (fill, floor fill, floor). Accordingly, the approach to estimating minimum numbers of individuals was something of a 'middle road' approach. Although both of the above assumptions might occasionally be violated, this approach probably led to more realistic estimates than either a minimal (site as a unit) or maximal (individual excavation units as units) approach.

Of the identifiable mammalian remains, cottontail rabbit (*Sylvilagus* sp.), black-tailed prairie dog (*Cynomys ludovicianus*), and black-tailed jackrabbit (*Lepus californicus*) are numerically dominant. Together they make up nearly 78 percent of the number of elements identified to genus level and slightly more than 50 percent of the estimated minimum number of individuals. Cottontails are the most numerous species with 60 bones representing a minimum of 11 individuals (Table 3.2). Most of these rabbits are probably desert cottontails (*Sylvilagus auduboni*), but a few are recognizably larger individuals and may be from the larger eastern cottontail (*S. floridanus*). Both species occur in the general vicinity of the site, but *S. floridanus* is mainly limited to the mountainous areas. It is possible that even the large specimens are of *S. auduboni*, inasmuch as both Findley and others (1975) and Hoffmeister and Lee (1963) note that members of this species are unusually large in this geographic area.

Prairie dogs are the next most abundant species, with 50 elements representing a minimum of 11 individuals. It is possible some bones of the skeletally similar rock squirrel, *Spermophilus* (*Citellus*) *variegatus*, are included here, but all major skull fragments are definitely of *Cynomys*. Jackrabbit bones are noticeably less frequent than the other two species (20 elements, 6 MNI) and are found in a variety of proveniences. Perhaps some of the remains of these three species represent postoccupational intrusions, but occasional burned bones and the general disarticulation of remains suggest that most of this material is cultural and represents food debris.

The only other rodent of moderate abundance (12 elements) is the pocket gopher (*Thomomys bottae*). Probably the bones represent postoccupational intrusives into the site; none show any burning or other cultural alteration. This observation is not to suggest that gophers were not procured and eaten at the site, but merely to note that they may be overrepresented. Four bones of woodrats (*Neotoma*) were recorded, three femurs and an innominate. No attempt at species identification was made, but on the basis of current distributions, they are most likely white-throated woodrats (*N. albigula*).

One femur in Room 2, Floor Fill may have been from the large banner-tailed kangaroo rat. The bone was incomplete and in poor condition and may instead be from an unidentified member of the squirrel family. A few additional elements were noted as possibly being from the squirrel family (other than the prairie dog), but none could be positively identified.

The only two elements of carnivores identified were the partial shaft of a tibia of an immature dog (Pit House 2 Fill) and a mandible of a raccoon (*Procyon lotor*; Room 2 Fill). The dog identification is uncertain and it is possible that it is a tibia from a young artiodactyl. The raccoon is definite, however, and shows at least some exploitation of riverine habitats. Some unidentifiable pieces may include other carnivore remains.

Large game animals are nearly evenly split between deer (probably 9 elements, 5 MNI) and pronghorn (9 elements, 4 MNI). Although this is only a small number of identifiable bones, there are an additional 21 elements that could be identified as artiodactyls but for which genus could not be determined. Moreover, there is a large quantity of bones in the 'unidentifiable medium-large mammal' category, the majority of which are probably the poorly preserved remains of deer or pronghorn. A surprisingly high proportion of both unidentifiable and identifiable fragments show heavy burning, either charred black or calcined white. For example, more than one-third of the unidentifiable medium large fragments were burned. This is a high percentage, compared to trash from the Anasazi area. This trend toward high percentage of burned remains apparently extends to all major proveniences at the site, and it may in part account for the rather low frequency of identifiable large mammal bones.

Another interesting aspect of the collection is the presence of young (less than one year old) and infant artiodactyl remains. At least three separate instances of such remains were noted and may indicate that the settlement inhabitants were not restricting their procurement to adult and young adult animals. At least some of the mature deer bones are recognizably smaller than most mule deer and are probably indicative of the smaller and more riverine white-tailed deer (*Odocoileus virginianus*). None of the deer elements could be clearly ascribed to mule deer (*O. hemionus*) and, accordingly, it is possible that all of the deer here are white-tails. The co-occurrence of pronghorn antelope with their preference for more arid, open lands again suggests exploitation of a diversity of habitats.

Tentative identifications of nonmammalian specimens by Dr. Paul Parmalee noted that of the avian bones from the site, there were two humeri, one from Room 4 Floor Fill that he thought was a mourning dove (*Zenaidura macroura*) and the other from Room 5 Fill that he noted as being "black-bird size." Of the two fish elements, Parmalee reported a fragment from Room 5 Floor to be a succor species. The one definite amphibian bone is a large humerus, presumably from a frog (Pit House 1 Fill). The five reptile bones are all vertebrae from a single snake from Pit House 1 Floor Fill.

PLANT REMAINS

Only one flotation sample was obtained, from the ashy fill of the firepit in Room 5 (Feature 12B). This sample was processed by Mollie Toll; it contained only five seeds, none of which were burned: two fragments of *Portulaca* sp. and three fragments of *Chenopodium berlandieri*.

COMPARABLE SITES

Villareal II is one of the few systematically excavated Salado sites in the Upper Gila. Comparable Salado sites, with systematic collections, include the Ormand and Riverside sites. Riverside was a small Salado farmstead next to a small Mimbres pueblo structure (Baker 1971). Ormand was much larger, town-sized, with 150 rooms (Wallace 1998).

The Salado architecture at Riverside (Chapter 4) consisted of cimiento walls, much like those at Villareal II, forming a small room block of least two and probably four rooms. Neither of the two excavated rooms had a hearth. A single subfloor inhumation resembled the one at Villareal II. A low proportion of Salado polychromes (about 1% of all sherds, much like Villareal) is compensated, perhaps, by the presence of a Gila Polychrome bowl, from a floor context. Like Villareal

II, Mimbres white wares outnumbered Salado polychromes by 126 to 19 in the Salado unit ("Complex A"; Baker 1971, Table 3).

Ormand consisted of four room blocks, each about 15 to 35 rooms, clustered around a plaza. A "ceremonial room" was excavated in the middle of the plaza. Two cremation cemeteries were located at the margins of the site. Each of the room blocks was up to six times larger than the Villareal II site and the presence of formal cemeteries and "ceremonial rooms" indicate a different kind of settlement than Villareal II or Riverside. Those small sites were farmsteads; Ormand was a town. Salado polychromes were much more prominent at Ormand, reaching almost 10 percent of all sherds (Wilson in Wallace 1998, Table 2). Although there was considerable admixture of Mimbres ceramics in the Villareal II assemblage, the range of later, fourteenth-century pottery at Villareal II matches almost exactly the ceramics recovered at the Ormand site (Wallace 1998).

Villareal II architecture also closely resembles that at the Ormand site, in several particulars. Wall construction was identical, with two or three rows of cimientos forming the bases of thin puddled adobe walls. Rooms at Villareal II averaged 162.6 square feet (14.45 square meters), somewhat smaller than the average Ormand room (16.05 square meters; Wallace 1998: 77, 117). Almost every excavated room at Ormand had a firepit (24 of 27; Wallace 1998), whereas 3 of 5 rooms at Villareal II had firepits. The construction and placement of firepits were similar at the two sites. About half of the rooms at Ormand also contained one or more mealing bins, a feature absent at Villareal II. Burials at Ormand were almost entirely urn cremations in well-defined extramural cemeteries; the single burial at Villareal II was a subfloor inhumation in Room 2 (like the Salado component at the Riverside site). Numerous doorways were in the Ormand room blocks. A possible break in the east wall of Room 5 at Villareal II may represent a door, but no preserved doorways were uncovered. At Villareal II, preserved walls were low, below the tops of the cimientos, and the low preservation of walls might have eliminated any evidence of the raised-sill doorways present at Ormand.

The large Ormand site had several unique or rare features not seen at Villareal; the only feature present at Villareal II that was not present or reported at Ormand was the possible granary platform (Unit B). In summary, the Villareal II ceramic assemblage resembles that at Ormand but with proportionately less Salado polychrome pottery. Architecturally, Villareal II appears to be a nearly identical smaller, attenuated version of the much larger Ormand.

DATING

The initial dating of Villareal II placed the main room block in the "Animas phase," a putatively transitional phase between the Mimbres phase (A.D. 1000–1150) and the Salado Cliff phase (A.D. 1300–1450; Lekson 1978b; Lekson and Klinger 1973). Subsequent rethinking amended that dating to the present scheme, with the pit houses dating to the Mangas or early Mimbres phase and the room block dating to the Salado Cliff phase (Lekson 1992a). New analyses, reported below, support that latter assessment.

Dating of the room block is not aided by absolute dates. Only one absolute date was obtained from Villareal II: a ^{14}C date from a wood beam fragment in the fill of Pit House 1. This specimen (N–1588) produced a calibrated one-sigma range date of A.D. 990–1160, two-sigma range 890–1230 (calibrated using OxCal 3.5). The one sigma range seems entirely conformable with Mimbres phase ceramics found throughout the excavated assemblage. The occurrence of Mimbres Boldface Black-on-white sherds on the floor of Pit House 1 (along with four sherds of Mimbres Classic Black-on-white) present the possibility that these earth-walled semisubterranean structures represent the chimerical Mangas phase (Lekson 1990a, 1999a). The two-sigma range of the date encompasses the entire range of both Mangas and Mimbres phases. The vast majority of the ceramic evidence and the one-sigma range both suggest that Pit Houses 1 and 2 were Mimbres phase structures.

Dating of the room block and other major features at Villareal II relies principally on ceramics, and the ceramic cross-dating of Villareal II has a history. At the time of excavation in 1972 (almost a decade before the 1981 publication of "A Reevaluation of the Mogollon-Mimbres Archaeological Sequence" by Roger Anyon, Patricia Gilman, and Steven LeBlanc, the dating of Mimbres Black-on-white was generally considered to extend from the twelfth through the early thirteenth century:

> The total range of tree-ring dates is from 1113 + to 1347. There is no good evidence for determining the beginning date of Mimbres Black-on-white, but it apparently persisted until some time after 1250. (Breternitz 1966: 86)

James Fitting (1972a: 21), the director of the Upper Gila Project, dated the "classic phase of the Mimbres sequence as that period between A.D. 1000 and A.D. 1200 (based on guess dates at present)." The beginning dates for Gila Polychrome were also, at that time, poorly known, but Charles Di Peso suggested pre–1300 dates for this type from Paquimé (Di Peso 1966 and in personal communications to me in 1972 and 1973). Thus, the co-occurrence of Mimbres Black-on-white and Gila Polychrome was taken as indicative of a temporal period intermediate between Mimbres and fully developed Salado. Gila Polychrome did not occur in every context at Villareal II, but Mimbres white wares were found throughout, and thus every context with Gila Polychrome also included Mimbres white wares with the Mimbres consistently in the majority.

The posited period intermediate between Mimbres and Salado was termed "Animas phase" in the Cliff Valley (Fitting 1972a) and southwestern New Mexico (see Hegmon and others 1999; and Lekson 1992b for a review of the Animas phase). Based on its Mimbres–Salado ceramic assemblage, Villareal II was originally assigned to the Animas phase (Lekson 1978b; Lekson and Klinger 1973), lacking absolute chronology but intermediate between purely Mimbres and purely Salado assemblages in the regional sequence.

The subsequent redating of Mimbres Black-on-white to A.D. 1000–1150 (Anyon and others 1981), and the nearly universal negative reaction to pre–1300 Gila Polychrome at Paquimé (and the redating of that site; Dean and Ravesloot 1993), made the "Animas phase" assignment of Villareal II difficult to sustain. Recent suggestions that Mimbres Black-on-white survived into the early thirteenth century in the Black Range (Hegmon and others 1999; M. Nelson 1999) do not alter the case: there appears to be a 100- to 150-year gap between the end of Mimbres Black-on-white at 1150 and the beginning of Gila Polychrome after 1300. Later publications (Le Blanc 1980; Lekson 1992b) reevaluated Villareal II and concluded that there were at least two separate occupations: a Mangas or Mimbres occupation with subterranean Pit Houses 1 and 2 and a much later Salado (or "Cliff phase") occupation represented by the five-room pueblo.

However, Mimbres pottery is pervasive in every context at the room block and far outnumbers later Salado types. Reanalysis of the collections, however, supports the two-component interpretation. Although several undecorated types can be assigned to either Mimbres or Salado occupations, the vast majority of nonpainted sherds are not temporally specific (for example, plain brown wares, which make up about 60% of the total collection). Therefore, this analysis focuses solely on

the two decorated series: Mimbres white wares and Salado polychromes. Mimbres sherds were densely distributed in and around Pit Houses 1 and 2, as demonstrated by the systematic surface survey. These earlier sherds could have been incorporated into construction and deposition by the later Salado occupation, an interpretation that might have been easily reached if the Mimbres sherds did not outnumber Salado sherds by a ratio of about 10:1. The remarkable preponderance of Mimbres over Salado decorated sherds made it difficult to dismiss Mimbres sherds as simple "mixture." This ratio can be understood, perhaps, by examining two processes: differential decorated ceramic production and sherd size.

Mimbres assemblages characteristically include higher proportions of decorated pottery than post-Mimbres assemblages. For example, in the Cliff Valley, the Mimbres Saige-McFarland site ceramic assemblage was between 25 to 30 percent painted decorated sherds (Lekson 1990a), whereas at the Salado Ormand site only about 12 percent of the assemblage was painted decorated sherds (Wallace 1998). These differences appear to exist in most of the Salado sites in southwestern New Mexico (for example, Nelson and LeBlanc 1986). All other things being equal, if the Mimbres and Salado components at Villareal II represent essentially identical groups and settlement occupation spans, we might expect two to three times as many Mimbres white ware sherds as Salado polychrome sherds.

Site formation processes affect the number and distribution of sherds. Sherds from the earlier Mimbres component would have been subjected to additional decades of natural and artificial effects, bioturbation and breakage. These processes should be demonstrable by sherd size; that is, Mimbres sherds should be smaller than Salado sherds, and this appears to be the case. Sherds were weighed, and average weights by type and context were computed. For the entire assemblage, Mimbres white ware sherds averaged 3.52 g weight (sd = 1.03, N = 430) and Salado polychrome sherds averaged 6.31 g weight (sd = 2.28, N = 42). The two wares differ in vessel form and manufacture, but insofar as weight reflects sherd size, Salado sherds were almost twice as large as Mimbres sherds at Villareal II.

Average sherd sizes varied among architectural units. Mimbres sherds averaged between 2.65 g and 3.82 g in all units except Pit House 2, where Mimbres sherds were nearly twice that weight at 5.68 g. The few Salado sherds in pit house contexts were small, averaging 1.0 g, but Salado sherds in Rooms 2 and 5 averaged more than 8 g. Salado sherds in other contexts generally varied between 3.96 g and 4.75 g in average weight. Thus the largest Mimbres sherds were in pit house contexts and the largest Salado sherds were in Rooms 2 and 5.

These measures of differential decorated pottery production and sherd size are crude, but together they suggest that ratios of 10:1 Mimbres to Salado sherds may accurately reflect two discrete, generally similar occupations of the Villareal II site. If Mimbres assemblages contained three times the amount of decorated pottery as Salado assemblages, and if Mimbres sherds through site formation processes were broken into twice as many comparable Salado sherds (that is, Mimbres sherds were reduced to half the size of Salado sherds), then we would expect ratios of about 6:1, not wildly different from the observed ratio. Again, these measures are simple estimates, but they do support the notion of two separate components.

Thus, the two components (pit houses and room block) at Villareal II appear to represent two distinct chronological periods, Mimbres and Salado. The "northeast" surface concentration hints at a much earlier component, but current data are insufficient to clarify its nature. Unit A, with Chupadero Black-on-white in its fill and Mimbres Boldface Black-on-white on its floors, may be a small Mangas phase room block predating the Mimbres pit houses, but the small sherd sample makes this assignment problematic. In sum, two main occupations seem well attested by architecture, stratigraphy, the ^{14}C date and ceramics: two Mangas or Mimbres phase pit houses and the five-room Salado pueblo.

CHAPTER FOUR

The Sites in Context

Villareal II and Dutch Ruin represent two extremes in Salado site size: Villareal II had five rooms and Dutch Ruin had 150 rooms or more. This chapter attempts to put these two very different sites into eastern Salado contexts through discussions of (1) chronology and settlement duration, (2) settlement pattern, and (3) ceramic assemblages.

CHRONOLOGY AND DURATION

A single eleventh-century ^{14}C date from Villareal II came from a Mimbres pit structure and not from the Salado component at that site. There are no absolute dates from Dutch Ruin, and no preserved materials that might produce such a date. Only a few absolute dates pertain to the Upper Gila Salado, and most are fraught with the difficulties expected from archaeological materials so unevenly collected. There are five tree-ring dates and six archaeomagnetic dates.

Tree-ring dates are reported from three Upper Gila Salado sites. Two cutting dates of A.D. 1243 were derived from unknown contexts at the Hilltop Ruin on Duck Creek (Lekson 1992b); Hilltop was a large multi-component settlement that contained sizable Mimbres and Salado occupations. The mid-thirteenth-century date would almost certainly not relate to the Mimbres phase occupation, which is generally considered to have ended between A.D. 1130 and 1150. If these two cutting dates are associated with the Salado occupation, then the Hilltop Ruin is one of the earliest Salado sites in the Upper Gila or, indeed, anywhere in the Salado world. There is a limited Tularosa phase presence in the Cliff Valley (at the Villareal III site, Appendix A) and the two A.D. 1243 dates may have come from an unsuspected Tularosa phase component at Hilltop; however, Tularosa Black-on-white and Tularosa phase components are rare in the Upper Gila region. The third tree-ring date is a noncutting date of A.D. 1342 that came from Room 31 at the Ormand site (Wallace 1998: 412). Two more cutting dates at A.D. 1380 were obtained from room contexts at Kwilleylekia Ruins (Robinson and Cameron

1991: 23). Thus there are cutting dates from Upper Gila Salado sites that span an interval from A.D. 1243 to 1380, although the earlier dates are of uncertain context.

Two archaeomagnetic dates from Riverside were collected by Robert DuBois in the 1970s, and they have never been recalibrated. I learned from Thomas Windes and Jeff Eighmy in 2001 that no data on these samples are currently available. These dates are intriguing, however. A hearth in a semisubterranean structure at the Riverside site produced dates of A.D. 1155 ± 24 and 1175 ± 23 (Lekson 1992a, Table 5.3), surprisingly late for the Mimbres component and probably too early for the Salado occupation of that site. Two dates analyzed by Jeff Eighmy were procured from the Dinwiddie site by Ben Nelson; these were reported as A.D. 1330 ± 13 (from a hearth in Room 26, House 2) and A.D. 1240–1355 (from a burned wall in Room 9, House 2; Nelson and LeBlanc 1986, Table 5.1). Rumors of archaeomagnetic dates in the late fifteenth century from hearths at Kwilleylekia remain, despite my best efforts to track them down, unsubstantiated. I mention them here only to alert future researchers that, once upon a time, there were strange stories about very late occupations at Red Ellison's site.

The two mid-thirteenth-century tree-ring dates from unknown contexts at Hilltop Ruin are problematically early for Salado, particularly since Pinto Polychrome (the earliest of the Salado polychrome series) is rare or absent at Upper Gila Salado sites. Those two tree-ring dates, each at A.D. 1243, raise the specter of early Salado polychromes in the Chihuahuan desert (Di Peso 1976; LeBlanc and Nelson 1976), an argument rejected by most Salado archaeologists. Two tree-ring dates at A.D. 1380 obtained from Kwilleylekia are more comfortable in the accepted span of the later Salado polychromes. Ceramics indicate that, whatever its beginning dates, Upper Gila Salado certainly extended through the fourteenth century and perhaps into some portion of the fifteenth century. In a conversation with Richard Ellison in 1972, he hinted that sixteenth-century pottery types were represented at Kwilleylekia. Thus, it seems safe to suggest that the Cliff phase in the Upper Gila region began in the late thirteenth or early fourteenth centuries and continued through the fourteenth century.

Without absolute dates for their Salado components, the most useful chronological data for Villareal II and Dutch Ruin come from ceramic cross-dating. Both sites have two readily identified ceramic assemblages: Mimbres and Salado.

The mixture of Mimbres and Salado sherds at Villareal II originally suggested a chronological position intermediate between the two (tentatively identified as "Animas phase"), but more secure dating of Mimbres white wares and Salado polychromes at other sites now demonstrates that the possibility of overlap between the two is remote. Mimbres component ceramics at Villareal II are conformable with the single ^{14}C date from the site at A.D. 990–1160 (one sigma). The Villareal II Salado assemblage, although small and containing both Tucson Polychrome and Tonto Polychrome, seems solidly fixed in the fourteenth century. It is unlikely that this small site, lacking middens or cemeteries, was occupied for very long. Salado at Villareal II seems far more likely to have been a short occupation in the middle to late fourteenth century.

The Dutch Ruin Salado whole vessels represent a late thirteenth- through fourteenth-century assemblage. The absence of late thirteenth-century Pinto Polychrome and the presence of late Escondida-style Tonto Polychrome indicate a later fourteenth-century date. However, several types well represented in the collection span the entire fourteenth century, and it is possible that the Dutch Ruin Salado component also spanned the fourteenth century, in contrast to Villareal II and the "short-term sedentism" of Mimbres Valley Salado sites (Nelson and LeBlanc 1986).

Salado and indeed all post-Mimbres horizons in the Upper Gila region are implicated in the notions of "short-term sedentism" (Nelson and LeBlanc 1986) and "fallow valley" mobility (Nelson 2000; Nelson and Anyon 1996). The basic concept behind both terms is one of short occupation with cycles of intraregional mobility among unoccupied agriculturally useful valleys.

Short-term sedentism (Nelson and LeBlanc 1986) was first applied to Mimbres Valley Salado settlements that lacked middens, numerous burials, and architectural modifications and reconstructions, features that, taken together, would indicate long occupations. Nelson (2000; Nelson and LeBlanc 1986) mentions that the Mimbres Valley Salado settlements might have been occupied for only a generation, in contrast to earlier Mimbres phase settlements with hundreds of burials, architectural remodeling and modification, and deep ceramic and chronological histories.

Short-term sedentism may have occurred in the Mimbres Valley, but several Upper Gila Salado settlements (including Dutch Ruin) almost certainly had longer, more substantial occupations. At Dutch Ruin, two midden areas were noted, but no details survive on their size or ceramic associations. The number of burials (at least 20 and as many as 30 in 15 Salado rooms) also suggests a long occupation. Extended occupations are also indicated at the Ormand settlement, with two large cremation cemeteries, middens, and architectural remodeling. At least one large room block at Ormand was built over Salado period trash fill, again suggesting a long duration.

> The occupation at Ormand may have extended over several generations, as suggested by remodeling episodes, extensive trash deposits, intensive corn production, location on the first terrace above excellent and abundant farmland, and the construction of a large communal ceremonial structure. (Wallace 1998: 402)

Short occupations, comparable to the Mimbres Valley situation, likely occurred at Villareal II and similar small settlements such as the Riverside site. These two small sites are without numerous burials or cemeteries, lack middens, and do not reveal architectural modifications and rebuilding. They appear to be short-lived farmsteads and might fit the short-term sedentism model but with an important difference: the Upper Gila farmsteads were located close to much larger, much longer occupied Salado settlements and must be viewed as part of a larger, longer-lasting settlement system.

Although the dating of Dutch Ruin and Villareal II cannot be more precisely fixed than the fourteenth century, Dutch Ruin must have been occupied for a significant span of that century, whereas the Villareal II settlement was much shorter lived.

SETTLEMENT PATTERNS

There are at least eight large Salado sites in the Upper Gila (Lekson 1992a, 2000). Sites with more than 100 rooms include Dutch Ruin, Ormand, Dinwiddie, LA 39261, and Kwilleylekia. Three other sites have 50 to 80 rooms: Hilltop, LA 39035, and Willow Creek (see Figs. 1.1, 1.3).

There appear to be only a few sites comparable in size to Villareal II. The Riverside Ruin (Baker 1971), also with a small Salado farmstead masked by a larger Mimbres occupation, and Villareal II raise the possibility that other small Salado farmsteads may be masked in survey by earlier Mimbres components. Riverside consisted of one small Salado room block (Complex A), a larger Mimbres room block (Complex B), and a poorly defined pit structure. Like Villareal II, Mimbres ceramics were predominant in almost every context, but in fact Complex A was a small Salado pueblo much like the one at Villareal II, with cimiento architecture of parallel upright cobbles forming the bases of puddled adobe walls. "When parts of this adobe were broken apart, one Mimbres Black-on-white sherd was found" (Baker 1971: 8), that is, Mimbres ceramics were incorporated into the later structure. A partial Gila Polychrome bowl was in one of the rooms in Complex A, which also contained a subfloor burial presumably associated with the Salado occupation. For the entire site, however, Mimbres series decorated ceramics outnumbered Salado series pottery by a ratio of almost 15 to 1 (Baker 1971, Table 4).

Riverside and Villareal II both demonstrate that small, short Salado occupations may have generated far fewer diagnostic sherds than small Mimbres components at the same site. Explanations for this dichotomy include differing (1) lengths of occupations, (2) sizes of populations, (3) ratios of painted vessels during the two phases, or (4) ceramic discard rates.

Out of 5,453 sherds collected in "grab" samples from the Upper Gila Survey, only 58 were Salado polychromes (50 Gila, 8 Tonto; Klinger 1975). The occurrence of only a few Salado polychrome sherds in surface collections at Mimbres sites might indicate a small farmstead like Riverside or Villareal II. Odd sherds of Gila Polychrome and other Salado types are not common in surface collections, but neither are they unknown. In the Cliff Valley, survey records reveal only three other Mimbres sites with a few Salado sherds, but they may well indicate small Salado farmsteads like Villareal II or Riverside: site G–24 (just upstream from Villareal II), site G–54 (just above the confluence of Mangas Creek and the Gila), and site G–71 (immediately upstream from the Saige-McFarland site). One or more of these three Mimbres sites probably had a small Salado component like Villareal II or Riverside, for a total of perhaps half-a-dozen small Salado farmsteads.

In the Redrock Valley, similarly, Salado polychromes were common at two large Salado sites (Dutch Ruin and LA 39035), but they were also present in small numbers at two large Mimbres sites (Redrock Village and the Redrock Cemetery Site; Lekson 1978a).

These two sites, at least, probably had small Salado components, perhaps like Villareal II and Riverside. Salado polychromes were almost entirely absent from other Redrock Valley sites. It appears that in Redrock the Salado population was highly aggregated into one large and one medium-sized settlement, with two or more affiliated small farmsteads.

Although Villareal II and Riverside were not unique, small homesteads were only a minor part of Salado settlement patterns in the Upper Gila (unlike the earlier Mimbres phase, during which small settlements were much more numerous). Clearly, the large majority of the Salado population was aggregated in large pueblos of 50 rooms or more, with most of the population residing in pueblos of 100 rooms or more.

Four large Salado sites along the Gila River are spaced at irregular intervals. In the Redrock Valley, Dutch Ruin and LA 39035 are the two major Salado sites (see Fig. 1.1). Dutch Ruin, with about 150 rooms, is located on a low terrace ridge in the middle of the main valley segment. LA 39035 is about 8 km (5 miles) downstream from Dutch Ruin. A short but well-defined narrows separates the main Redrock Valley from an isolated pocket of arable land just above the Lower Box; that is the setting of LA 39035, a medium-sized, 50–room Salado pueblo. LA 39035 is on a high terrace above the Gila River. Both Dutch Ruin and LA 39035 have substantial Mimbres components, and the ceramic sample from LA 39035 is both smaller and less diverse than the Dutch Ruin surface collections. However, our original field assessment was that LA 39035 (Animas phase) was earlier than Dutch Ruin (Salado phase; Lekson 1978a). Only excavation can verify that assessment.

The Redrock Valley is separated from the Cliff Valley by the long narrow Middle Box. Within the Cliff Valley, there was a single early Salado site (Ormand, with 100 rooms) and a single late Salado site (Kwilleylekia, with 200 rooms). Ormand was located on an isolated butte at the lower end of the Cliff Valley, just below the confluence of Bear Creek and Duck Creek with the Gila River (see Fig. 1.1), a spot with obvious strategic potential. Kwilleylekia, in contrast, was located on a low terrace just above the river in mid valley, about 7 km (4 miles) above Ormand.

Curiously, in both the Redrock and the Cliff valleys there appear to be pairs of large Salado sites. On the admittedly thin basis of surface ceramics, the smaller sites in the pairs date earlier than the larger sites. "Earlier" in this context might mean early fourteenth century; "later" could mean late fourteenth and early fifteenth century. The smaller, and presumably earlier settlements were located downstream from the larger, presumably later settlements at the lower end of valley segments or at strategic locations: LA 39035, thought to be earlier than Dutch Ruin, was located on a high terrace in an isolated valley segment; Ormand, definitely earlier than Kwilleylekia, was located on a butte at the confluence of several major streams. The larger, later settlements were located on low landforms, directly above the valley bottom, in the approximate middle or center of the valley.

It is possible that Villareal II, directly across the river from Kwilleylekia, predates that large town and may actually be contemporary with earlier Ormand. If so, Villareal II may represent a farmstead associated with Ormand in the then-empty upper Cliff Valley. Lacking absolute dates from the Salado occupation at Villareal II, this reconstruction is speculative, but it may explain the presence of a five-room farmstead so close to the large town of Kwilleylekia (see Appendix A, Fig. A.1). Villareal II seems too large for a field house, but too small for an independent village, hence it was probably a farmstead, presumably associated with a larger town community, possibly Ormand.

Three large Salado sites along Duck Creek are Dinwiddie, Hilltop, and LA 39261. Although there is even less information on their relative dating, the two early A.D. 1243 tree-ring dates come from Hilltop Ruin, so named because it sits atop an isolated low butte. A.D. 1243 represents a remarkably early date for Salado sites in any region; the potential importance of these dates is obvious but, in the absence of contextual data, problematic. LA 39261 and Dinwiddie, in contrast, are located on low terraces above the Duck Creek floodplain. Perhaps the pattern tentatively identified for the Cliff Valley and suggested for the Redrock Valley also pertains to Duck Creek: an early Salado village in a defensive or otherwise strategic setting and later Salado villages built closer to the floodplain and presumably to agricultural fields.

The foregoing discussion is highly speculative, extrapolating from the apparent Cliff Valley situation to more fragmentary observations in the Redrock and Duck Creek valleys. But the suggested patterns are consistent with the data and may indicate a medium-sized founder village in each valley, followed by the establishment of a larger, mature village at a short but appreciable distance from the original settlement.

Eighteenth-century explorers noted canals (and, of course, ruins) in the Cliff Valley, which was then called *Todos Santos* (Kessel 1971). Canal irrigation is strongly indicated for the Mimbres phase occupation of the Up-

per Gila (Lekson 1992b) and undoubtedly canal irrigation was a major factor in Salado subsistence as well. Small sites such as Villareal II and Riverside might represent caretaker stations along canals, but we lack identification of the probable canal diversion points or other key canal architecture with which these small settlements might have been associated.

In summary, Dutch Ruin was one of a half-dozen large Cliff phase Salado towns in the Upper Gila. Those towns may represent pairs of earlier and later settlements, in which case Dutch Ruin would have been the later counterpart of the earlier, more isolated, and defensive LA 39035. Villareal II, on the other hand, was a small Salado farmstead. Small farmsteads apparently were relatively rare in the Upper Gila, but their identification may be "masked" as later components at multicomponent Mimbres-Salado sites.

CERAMIC INTERPRETATIONS

Salado is nothing if not pottery. For ceramic comparisons and interpretations I use Southwestern ceramic typology as a common standard that cross-cuts the various reports and analyses discussed here. In so doing I assume that typological definitions and applications were relatively uniform in this region of New Mexico. This may be a big assumption, of course, but considering the distinctiveness of many of the types in question (Salado polychromes, Tucson Polychrome, Ramos Polychrome) it is a reasonably safe assumption for fourteenth-century painted or decorated wares. The nomenclature and typology (and the recovery and curation) of plain, undecorated pottery were clearly far less standardized, and those wares are not included in these observations.

Painted and decorated ceramics are discussed as "types"; for some distinctive and affiliated types the more generalized level of "wares" or "series of types" is used. For purposes of this presentation, the two levels of ceramic taxonomy are occasionally treated equivalently, I hope with no violence to their taxonomic utility. Whole vessel collections are emphasized, but the following discussion also includes systematic or semi-systematic sherd collections. Dutch Ruin and Villareal II are contrasted with Solomonsville (Tyberg 2000), Ormand (Wallace 1998), and Dinwiddie (Mills and Mills 1972) and (for comparison) I make some observations regarding three Mimbres Valley Salado sites (Nelson and LeBlanc 1986).

With the exception of the huge Solomonsville collection and the exceedingly few partial vessels from Villa-

Table 4.1. Frequency of Painted and Decorated Whole Vessels at Salado Sites in the Upper Gila River Region

Vessels	Dutch	Ormand	Solomons-ville	Dinwiddie
Mimbres Black-on-white	5			
Cibola Black-on-white	3	3		
Mesa Verde style B/W	1			
Chupadero Black-on-white	4			
El Paso Polychrome	7			2
Salado polychromes	22	20	61	20
Tucson Polychrome	7	1	5	4
Chihuahua polychromes	5			
Kwakina Polychrome			1	
White Mountain Red Ware	2		3	
Cliff White-on-red		1	1	9
Gila Black-on-red			5	1
Variety of red-on-brown			10	
Total	56	22	89	36

real II, whole vessel assemblages at all of these sites are roughly comparable (Table 4.1). Systematic surface collections from Dutch Ruin included about 2,500 sherds and Villareal II collections included about 4,900 sherds; collections from the other sites are much larger: Dinwiddie about 20,500 sherds, Ormand about 23,800 sherds, and the Mimbres Valley sites together about 20,000 sherds.

The number of different types and wares in an assemblage provides a rough measure of assemblage diversity. The range of decorated types (sherds and whole vessels) varies intriguingly from west to east. Western sites (Solomonsville, Dutch Ruin) each have about 25 decorated types (Tyberg 2000, Table 4–3). Both Solomonsville and Dutch Ruin are large sites, with large collections. Salado sites in the Cliff Valley are much more restricted in the range of decorated types represented: Ormand (which is not quite so large, but which has a large collection) has 10 decorated types (Wallace 1998), Dinwiddie (comparable to Ormand in size) has at least 7 but no more than 10 types (Mills and Mills 1972), and Villareal II has 11 decorated types. Willow Creek, in the Mangas Valley, is a large site with a small collection, which includes only two decorated types. Mimbres Valley Salado sites, relatively small in size but with large collections, have up to five decorated types represented (El Paso, Gila, Tonto, and Ramos polychromes and Chupadero Black-on-white; Nelson and LeBlanc 1986: 136–138).

The number of types may be a reflection of sample size, collection techniques, the length of occupations,

and the diversity of ceramics. Almost all these sites, large and small, are multicomponent and only one collection (from Willow Creek) could be considered small. In general, it appears that the number of decorated types present at Salado sites is higher in collections from the western Salado sites and lower from the eastern Salado sites on the Upper Gila. There is greater diversity in the range of decorated types in collections from western sites and less diversity in collections from eastern sites. This difference may simply reflect size: Solomonsville and Dutch Ruin are larger sites than the Cliff Valley sites. Ormand and Dinwiddie, however, are themselves very large sites with very large collections. Another explanation might be that there was a greater time depth at Solomonsville and Dutch Ruin. Solomonsville, in particular, might have been a major settlement in the pre-Classic Hohokam, Mimbres–Encinas, and Salado periods. But again, Ormand, Dinwiddie, and Villareal II were comparable; if not as dramatically "deep," they were all multicomponent sites. Tentatively then, the pattern appears to be more typological diversity in the west and less in the east. Whole vessel collections mirror that larger pattern, but fewer types are represented by whole vessels.

Solomonsville has the largest whole vessel collection and (by far) the widest range of types. Dutch Ruin is perhaps second in both numbers and variety; the range of types represented in whole vessel collections from other Salado sites is far more limited. This pattern might be attributable to sample size, particularly in the case of the very large collection from Solomonsville, but the whole vessel trends parallel similar patterns evident in the sherd assemblages.

More important, of course, than the number of different types identified in whole vessel and sherd collections are the particular types represented. The five most frequent painted or decorated types or series at Dutch Ruin are Salado polychromes, Tucson Polychrome, El Paso Polychrome, Chupadero Black-on-white, and Chihuahua polychromes.

Salado Polychromes

The common element of all Salado ceramic assemblages is Salado polychrome pottery. Gila Polychrome is well represented in the Dutch Ruin whole vessel collections, and there is one Tonto Polychrome vessel (Table 2.4), but Gila and Tonto polychromes make up only 0.8 percent (42 sherds) of the Villareal II excavated sample. At New Mexico Salado sites, Salado polychromes make up between 2 percent and 10 percent, with the lowest percentages at Mimbres Valley sites (Nelson and LeBlanc 1986, Table 1.2) and the highest percentages at the Cliff Valley sites of Dinwiddie (7%, Mills and Mills 1972) and Ormand (9.9%, Wilson in Wallace 1998, Table 2). Deposits at Dinwiddie and Ormand were not screened and may therefore be biased toward decorated sherds, but even so, Villareal II appears to represent the minimum proportion of Salado polychromes at any New Mexico Salado site. With the exception of one very small (1 g) sherd found in the floor fill of Pit House 2, all Salado polychrome sherds at Villareal II came from rooms, including floor contexts. Elsewhere, I summarized the contexts of Salado polychrome vessels at Salado sites in the upper Gila (Lekson 2000: 281); despite Dutch Ruin burials:

> Gila Polychrome vessels in the Safford and Cliff Valleys were usually found, not in burials, but in living rooms (i.e., rooms with hearths), typically a jar and perhaps a bowl with several nondecorated vessels, either on floors or (quite often) in what the excavators defined as roof fall.

There were five unidentified vessels (types are unknown) found singly on floors at Dutch Ruin; some of these may have been Salado polychromes. One presumed floor assemblage (Table 2.6, Context H) consists of two brown ware vessels. Context A represents a cluster of seven vessels, including four of Gila Polychrome, on the floor of Room 3; it is a clear exception to my generalization, above. Although records are incomplete, Context A appears to be the largest concentration of Salado polychromes as a floor assemblage at any Upper Gila Salado site. Context A, however, may be an unusual but not exceptional assemblage, when compared to other floor assemblages. At Ormand (which has by far the best data), floor assemblages with Salado polychromes generally consisted of one or two polychrome vessels, with or without one or two non-decorated vessels (Wilson in Wallace 1998, Table 23). Twenty-one whole-vessel floor assemblages had between one and four vessels of various types; eleven had no Salado polychromes; and assemblages that did have Salado polychromes included six assemblages with one polychrome vessel, three with two polychrome vessels, and one with three polychrome vessels. Viewed as a small, but normal, one-tailed statistical distribution, Context A at Dutch Ruin may represent an expectable occurrence. That is, if five or six rooms at Dutch Ruin had assemblages like Context A, it would be a statistical anomaly; but one assemblage like Context A is probably not remarkable.

For burial associations of Dutch Ruin Salado polychromes, only three possible inhumations are documented, two of which had Salado polychromes. It is likely that Salado polychromes were associated with many more (up to 20 or 30) inhumations, which, as noted above, would be a clear exception to the broad Upper Gila patterns.

Vessel forms in the Dutch Ruin Salado collections are well within the known range of Salado types, with the notable exception of Vessel 13 (Fig. 2.6), a rare Gila Polychrome "seed jar" (Crown 1994). Bowls tend to be small, but within the range of Salado vessels (with the exception of miniature bowl X–7 with its unusual double-headed bird depiction, not illustrated). The single exotic form, a submarine or football-shaped vessel, represents an infrequent but widespread Salado form (Crown 1994).

Dutch Ruin whole vessel design layouts fit within the Salado canon (Crown 1994), but the frequencies of certain layouts are, perhaps, unusual. Four bowls had banded designs, nine had offset quartered layouts, one had a repeat motif, and one had a center-focused layout. In Crown's "borderland" distribution area (which includes the Upper Gila), about 50 percent of the vessels she analyzed had banded designs, whereas less than 10 percent were offset quartered, that is, banded designs were five times as frequent as offset quartered designs (Crown 1994, Table 5.5). In this respect, Dutch Ruin appears anomalous, but the size of the collection precludes definitive conclusions.

Assignable design styles on Dutch Ruin Salado vessels included six Roosevelt (stage 3) and five Pinedale (stage 4) styles and one Escondida style. In Crown's borderland distribution area, Escondida and Pinedale (stage 5), which was absent at Dutch Ruin, each made up almost one-fourth of all designs. In the larger borderland sample, Crown discerned that Roosevelt (stage 3) and Pinedale (stage 4) styles each equalled only about 10 percent. The Dutch Ruin Salado vessels thus do not reflect the larger borderland patterns, but whether because of geography, chronology, or simple chance is uncertain.

Designs at Dutch Ruin suggest a relatively late place in the poorly defined Salado sequence. Both the Pinedale (stage 4) style and particularly the Escondida style are thought to be late. An important typological observation, relevant to dating, is the absence of Pinto Polychrome, the earliest Salado polychrome type, at every Upper Gila site considered here, except Dutch Ruin (Table 2.1), where it was listed as present by Fortenberry and Bennett (1968). Pinto Polychrome was not observed in the 1974 surface collections nor in the present analysis of whole vessels from Dutch Ruin.

Tucson Polychrome and Maverick Mountain Polychrome

Tucson Polychrome and Maverick Mountain Polychrome are well represented at Solomonsville and at all the Upper Gila sites: Dutch Ruin, Ormand, and Dinwiddie, and four sherds of Tucson Polychrome came from room contexts at Villareal II. These types, in contrast, are entirely absent from the Mimbres Valley sites. Tucson and Maverick Mountain polychromes did, occasionally, reach farther east than the Mimbres Valley; at least one bowl is reported just north of El Paso, Texas, in association with Chihuahua polychromes (Moore and Wheat 1951), and more than 100 sherds of Tucson Polychrome were found at Paquime (Di Peso and others 1974: 154).

El Paso Polychrome

El Paso Polychrome is solidly present at all sites considered here as both whole vessels and sherds, except (strangely) at Ormand. At Ormand, there were no whole vessels and only 12 sherds of El Paso Polychrome, compared to 40 sherds and 7 vessels at Dutch Ruin and 10 sherds from both pit house and room contexts at Villareal II. The virtual absence of El Paso Polychrome at Ormand is odd because this pottery spans the entire temporal range of Gila Polychrome, which is well represented at Ormand. El Paso Polychrome is widely distributed throughout southern and southwestern New Mexico and is well represented at nearby Dinwiddie in the form of large El Paso Polychrome jars and as sherds at much smaller sites such as Villareal II.

Chupadero Black-on-white

Chupadero Black-on-white pottery appears to be significantly better represented in the Dutch Ruin collections than in collections from other Upper Gila Salado sites, with the exception of Villareal II. There were four whole vessels of this type at Dutch Ruin; there were no whole vessels of Chupadero Black-on-white at Solomonsville, Ormand, or Dinwiddie, and only one vessel fragment from the Mimbres Valley Salado sites. At Dutch Ruin, 28 sherds were recovered in the 1974 sample. There was only one sherd of this type at Ormand and (apparently) none at Dinwiddie. Significantly, there

was no Chupadero Black-on-white identified at Solomonsville in its small, nonsystematic, but highly diverse sample. There were 75 sherds of Chupadero Black-on-white in the three Mimbres Valley sites (out of nearly 20,000 sherds); presumably, some of these 75 were part of one incomplete vessel, but sherds of Chupadero Black-on-white came from all three Mimbres Valley sites (Nelson and LeBlanc 1986). Villareal II was an exception to the dearth of Chupadero at Upper Gila sites: of the 37 sherds (almost as many sherds as were recovered of the Salado polychromes), about one-third came from pit houses and two-thirds came from room contexts. Chupadero Black-on-white stands out as an important element of the Dutch Ruin whole vessel and sherd assemblages, in contrast to other large Upper Gila Salado sites.

Chihuahua Polychromes

A particularly intriguing aspect of the Dutch Ruin whole vessel collection is that the Chihuahua polychromes were represented by five vessels. Other whole vessel collections (including the large and diverse Solomonsville collection) lack Chihuahua decorated types, although sherds of it were recovered at most sites (excluding Villareal II). At Dutch Ruin, two Chihuahua vessels were unambiguously associated with Gila Polychrome and Chupadero Black-on-white in a subfloor adult(?) inhumation (Table 2.6, Context D).

Although there were only 7 sherds of Chihuahua polychromes in the approximately 2,449 sherds from the 1974 controlled surface collections from Dutch Ruin, it is instructive to contrast Dutch Ruin totals to the numbers of Chihuahua sherds from the much larger collections at Ormand, the Mimbres Valley Salado sites, and Dinwiddie. These collections range in size from 20,000 to 24,000 sherds. There was only 1 sherd representing the Chihuahua polychromes at Ormand (Wallace 1998), only 3 sherds at the Mimbres Valley Salado sites (Nelson and LeBlanc 1986), and 35 sherds at Dinwiddie (Mills and Mills 1972). Thus, in collections with ten times the number of sherds as Dutch Ruin, Chihuahua sherds were either rarer (Ormand and the Mimbres Valley sites) or no more than five times as frequent (Dinwiddie). Sherds representing the Chihuahua polychromes were present at other Salado sites, but at the Dutch Ruin, whole vessels were recovered. Four Ramos Polychrome vessels and one Villa Ahumada Polychrome vessel stand in remarkable contrast to the near absence of Chihuahua polychrome vessels at other Upper Gila Salado sites.

Other Ceramic Types

Other ceramic types that appear important at other sites but are absent or nearly absent from the Dutch Ruin whole vessel collections and Villareal II sherd collections are Cliff White-on-red, Gila Black-on-red, and Salado-era red-on-brown pottery. These types are distinctive, and their absence is probably not due to lack of recognition by the analysts.

Cliff White-on-red seems to be largely limited to Cliff Valley sites, such as Ormand (Wilson in Wallace 1998), with possibly one example in the large Solomonsville collection (Tyberg 2000). Gila Black-on-red is well represented at Solomonsville and may be represented by a single vessel at Dinwiddie (which might be Wingate or another White Mountain black-on-red), but seems otherwise absent from Upper Gila Salado sites. Salado-era red-on-brown pottery may include Encinas Red-on-brown, San Carlos Red-on-brown, and Tanque Verde Red-on-brown; these types appear to be limited to Solomonsville and (presumably) the Safford Valley and are largely absent from the Redrock and Cliff valleys. These types are not represented in either vessels or sherds at Ormand, Dinwiddie, and the Mimbres Valley sites. They are absent from the Dutch Ruin whole vessel and 1974 surface collections, but Fortenberry and Bennett (1968) reported sherds of Encinas Red-on-brown and San Carlos Red-on-brown at Dutch Ruin.

In summary, the excavated sherd collections at Villareal II are notable for the presence of unusually high numbers of Chupadero Black-on-white sherds and the absence of Cliff White-on-red and Gila Red-on-black. The painted and decorated types at Villareal II are segregated between the two components (Mimbres pit houses, Salado rooms) as follows: Mimbres Black-on-white is present in every context; Tularosa Black-on-white occurred exclusively in pit house contexts (see Villareal I, Appendix A); Salado polychromes, Tucson Polychrome or Maverick Mountain Polychrome, and Socorro Black-on-white were solely in room contexts (with the exception of one small sherd of Gila Polychrome from Pit House 2 Fill); Chupadero Black-on-white and El Paso Polychrome appeared in both pit house and room contexts. In contrast, the whole vessel assemblage from Dutch Ruin is remarkable for the presence of Chupadero Black-on-white and Ramos Polychrome vessels, for the absence of Cliff White-on-red and Gila Black-on-red, and for the use of Salado Chihuahua polychromes in burial contexts. With these understandings of Upper Gila Salado, we now move to a survey of current, competing models of Salado. Was Salado a cult? A migration? A movable feast?

CHAPTER FIVE

Salado with a Grain of Salt

Four blindfolded archaeologists grope along an elephant, named "Salado," on the cover of *Proceedings of the Second Salado Conference* (Lange and Germick 1992). One holds the thin, ropelike tail; another tries the circumference of a tree-trunk leg; the third grasps the reptilian, squirming trunk; and the last sniffs a giant pile of dung. Each defines the elephant by that part they chanced to encounter: a rope, a tree, a snake, or something formless and fetid. None can form a true image of the whole, which is, of course, much more than those several parts.

In archaeology, we call this *systematics*: the naming and identifying of spatio-temporal units and determining their degree of relatedness. Salado may be profoundly ceramic–Salado boils down to pots–but its systematics go beyond pottery to measure also time and space. We do well with time: tree-rings and accelerators keep us honest. Space, however, is a problem. We typically work in smaller units of space than the phenomenon we study; we see only the tail, the tusk, the trunk, the leg of the beast.

The archaeologists-and-elephant cartoon (created by Carol Ellick and Richard Lange) was inspired by John Godfrey Saxe's famous poem, "The Blind Men and the Elephant." Saxe retold a parable from the *Udana*, a scripture of the Indian subcontinent. One anonymous translation of the original concludes with the Buddha dispensing a bit of uplifting verse:

O how they cling and wrangle, some who claim
For preacher and monk the honored name!
For, quarreling, each to his view they cling.
Such folk see only one side of a thing.

While there is little honor to be gained from wrangling about Salado, I fasten a quarrel on its systematics. It seems, to me, that we too often see only one side of a thing: our side of the state line. Nelson and Anyon's (1996) post-Mimbres "fallow valleys" end neatly at the state and national borders of southwestern New Mexico. Jeffery Clark's (2001) Salado migrations fit conveniently within the Grand Canyon State. The ancient Southwest seems remarkable congruent with modern political boundaries: curious.

Nelson, Anyon, and Clark venture outside the lines in other analyses. When we cross modern political boundaries (or conventional archaeological regions), we distinguish that act as "macro-regional analysis," an exceptional, daring scale. If there is no honor in wrangling about Salado, that stain spreads from the larger issue of *larger issues*; there is, alas, little glory in thinking big. Smaller is safer: big pictures are exponentially vulnerable to *falsum in uno, falsum in omnibus* rejection. But our various local Salados are clearly limbs and members of a very large elephant, and the elephant itself is a voucher of even bigger things. To understand Salado, we *must* think big: exceptional, unconventional large scales must become our norm.

For five decades, safe small scales have dominated Southwestern archaeology. Macro-regional analyses were only rarely attempted, most notably by David Wilcox and, for Salado, by Patricia Crown, among a very few others. I am delighted—we should all be delighted—at the recent bloom of macro-regional analyses in Southwestern archaeology, including the efforts by Nelson, Anyon, and Clark. Smaller is safer but bigger is better. Even bigger will be even better. Zoom out!

In this chapter, I discuss Salado systematics insofar as they impinge on the Upper Gila. I then place the Salado of the Upper Gila in a larger context.

CULTURAL SYSTEMATICS

It seems safe to assign Dutch Ruin to the Cliff phase Salado, with an earlier Mimbres phase component. Despite a convoluted history of interpretations (briefly recounted in Chapter 4), the cultural systematics of Villareal II seem, today, to be fairly straightforward. Pit Houses 1 and 2 and Unit A are Mangas or early Mimbres phase, and the room block of five rooms can be assigned to the Cliff phase. At both sites, there are ceramic hints of even earlier components. Those systematics come with a price: the labels we use reflect our underlying ideas about ancient dynamics.

Four models of the cultural systematics, with differing implications for Upper Gila Salado, were briefly introduced in Chapter 1. The origins of Upper Gila Salado have been variously attributed: (1) to Paquime (Di Peso 1976; LeBlanc and Nelson 1976; Nelson and LeBlanc 1986); (2) to intrusions of peoples from the Mogollon Highlands (Lindsay and Jennings 1968); (3) to local populations evolving in place (Fitting and others 1982; Lekson and Klinger 1973); and (4) to the regional development of "short-term sedentism" and "fallow valley" mobility (Nelson and Anyon 1996; Nelson and LeBlanc 1986). Local or regional evolutionary development are both compatible with Crown's (1994) interpretation of Salado as a cult adopted across a wide area by local populations. The first two of the four models (Paquime and Mogollon Highlands) imply discontinuity; the last two (local or regional evolutions) imply continuity. These arguments are now evaluated with new information from Dutch Ruin, Villareal II, and other Salado sites of the Upper Gila region.

Paquime and Salado Discontinuity

Paquime and the larger Casas Grandes region have been implicated in Salado origins in general (Di Peso 1976) and in Cliff phase origins in particular (LeBlanc and Nelson 1976; Nelson and LeBlanc 1986). Both arguments were founded on Di Peso's original dating of Paquime that suggested Salado polychromes at that site were decades earlier than similar types in the Salado "heartland." That dating has been convincingly reevaluated (Dean and Ravesloot 1993), and the consensus dating of Paquime places that site as contemporary with and not earlier than Salado and Cliff phase sites such as Dutch Ruin and Villareal II. Thus Paquime seems untenable as progenitor of Salado and the Cliff phase. However, at least some Upper Gila Salado settlements had close ties to Paquime, and the nature of those ties is a matter of some controversy.

Surface ceramics and survey data from 1974 suggested that Dutch Ruin was the only major Salado site in the Redrock Valley, and large quantities of Redrock serpentine at Paquime suggested that Dutch Ruin may have had an unusually close relationship with that great southern city (Lekson 1978a, 1982, 1992a). Serpentine was an important import at Paquime. Dutch Ruin was approximately 6 km (not quite 4 miles) from the serpentine source; the next nearest village contemporary with Paquime (that is, Ormand) was 25 km (15.5 miles) distant, with the rugged Middle Box between. Because of its close and seemingly exclusive proximity to the serpentine, it is plausible that Dutch Ruin was linked by trade, at least, to Paquime. This is reciprocally demonstrated by the Chihuahua polychromes in the Dutch Ruin whole vessel collections, a Chihuahuan ceramic presence that was perplexingly thin in the 1974 surface collections (Lekson 1992a: 20).

This interpretation was challenged by Laurel Wallace (1998) in her report on the Ormand Ruin. She couched the question as an aspect of Mogollon (northern) versus Paquime (southern) models of Salado origins, but then extended the suggested association of Dutch Ruin and Paquime to a far more general claim that Dutch Ruin's connections to Paquime somehow supported the "southern" model of Salado origins. That was not the intent of the sources she cited (Lekson 1978a and 1992a). Wallace (1998: 409–410) wrote:

> The Dutch Ruin to the south of Ormand, in the Middle Gila River box, and by extension the Cliff Valley, have been linked to Paquime because of its location [close] to a well-known serpentine source near Redrock, New Mexico. This suggestion is tenuous at best. Although Paquime did have many objects from this serpentine source location, including stockpiled serpentine in unworked form, it is unclear how this material was obtained and what role the Salado presence along the Gila River had to do with it . . . . Until known sources of Paquime production, such as copper bells and macaws, as well as a stronger presence of Chihuahuan ceramics, are found at Ormand or other Upper Gila Valley Salado sites, the southern model for the origin and development of the Salado phenomenon does not hold for this region.

The claim of Paquime origins was never made for Dutch Ruin, but the remarkable quantities of Redrock serpentine at Paquime do suggest strong ties between Paquime and Dutch Ruin, the largest contemporary town in the Redrock Valley. Even more positive linkages between Paquime and the Salado world (and, perhaps, Dutch Ruin) are spectacularly evident in large quantities of Gila Polychrome, almost 50 uniformly sized bowls that were found in the same rooms as the bulk of the serpentine at Paquime (Lekson 2000: 284–285). Similarities of rim form and compositional analysis link Gila Polychrome at Paquime to Gila Polychrome in Upper Gila sites. If Gila Polychrome pottery was imported into Paquime, it is more likely, based on formal and compositional grounds, to have come from the Upper Gila region than from other Salado subregions (Lekson 2000: 278–282). Conversely, it is likely that the Ramos Polychrome pottery found in Upper Gila sites was produced in or around Paquime rather than in the Upper Gila (Woosely and Olinger 1993). Wallace (1998) apparently extrapolated from the scarcity of Chihuahua polychromes at the Ormand site to a more general assumption that Chihuahua polychromes were absent at Upper Gila Salado sites. That situation has been suggested for the Mimbres Valley: "Chihuahua polychromes, which are relatively common during the Black Mountain phase, are all but absent during the Cliff phase" (Nelson and LeBlanc 1986: 246). However, Chihuahua polychromes were present in small amounts *both* at "Black Mountain" (Ravesloot 1979, Table 2) and in the Cliff phase (Nelson and LeBlanc 1986, Table 7.5) and in comparably small amounts at every Upper Gila Salado site for which we have ceramic information (see Chapters 2 and 4).

The Dutch Ruin whole vessel assemblage (Chapter 2) certainly supports the previously suggested strong association of Dutch Ruin and Paquime, with Chihuahua polychrome vessels found in direct association with Salado polychrome vessels. Perhaps these vessels qualify as the required "stronger presence of Chihuahuan ceramics" (Wallace 1998: 410) at Dutch Ruin, and the suggestion that Dutch Ruin and Paquime were closely linked can be promoted to something stronger than merely "tenuous." At the same time, it is clear that Dutch Ruin was not a cultural "outlier" of Paquime.

Di Peso's claims for Paquime and the Salado are ignored today, but there was something between the two. Casa Grande and Casas Grandes were two ends of an axis stretching 500 km across the southern deserts (a geographic circumstance noted by several archaeologists, among them Lekson 2000). For one brief shining moment in the ancient Southwest, there may have been two contemporary entities of sufficient size and complexity for us to think seriously about peer-polity interactions. Or perhaps not: the dynamics between Paquime and the Phoenix Basin remain to be defined. We will never know, of course, unless we look: another question ripe for large-scale thinking, with all its attendant dangers and difficulties. Areas in between, like the Upper Gila, should loom large in the Big Picture.

The Mogollon Highlands and Salado Discontinuity

The Cliff Valley and Upper Gila have long been recognized as a possible Salado "colony" (Lindsay and Jennings 1968), that is, an empty area in which Salado towns arose through in-migration (Lekson 2000). Although the nature of Salado in its putative "heartland" is a matter of ongoing and intense debate (Dean 2000), the chronology of this argument is at least possible, unlike the Paquime "southern" scheme.

Salado sites in the Upper Gila region appear in areas that were apparently nearly or entirely devoid of population. The effort by Hegmon and others (1999, Figs. 3, 4) to untangle post-Mimbres culture history in the U.S. Chihuahuan desert assists us in understanding the later prehistory of the Upper Gila by demonstrating the relative or even absolute lack of population in the late twelfth and thirteenth centuries. This "gap," unfortunately, appears to be projected to the Safford Valley where large pueblo sites with twelfth- and thirteenth-century ceramic assemblages are well known (Brown 1973). Perhaps the arbitrary truncation of the "Mimbres Region" at state and international boundaries caused this unsuitable distortion. However, the near or total absence of population in the Upper Gila region during the late twelfth and thirteenth centuries is largely correct, based on survey data (Lekson 1990a, 1992a, 1992b). Several absolute dates from the late twelfth and mid-thirteenth century (Chapter 4) suggest either a thin thirteenth-century Tularosa phase presence at a handful of Upper Gila sites such as Villareal III and perhaps Hilltop Ruin or, less certainly, earlier beginnings for Salado than would be suggested by ceramic cross-dating.

If the Upper Gila region was largely empty in the thirteenth century, the large Salado settlements of the fourteenth century cannot be explained by local evolution or changes in material culture. A sizable population must have immigrated into the Cliff and Redrock Valleys. Although the architecture of the Cliff Valley Salado sites more closely resembles desert technologies than Mogollon Highland technologies, the ceramics strongly favor a Mogollon Highland origin for these immigrants. C. Dean Wilson, in the Ormand report (Wallace 1998: 262–263), concludes his meticulous analysis of 23,805 sherds and 83 whole vessels with some general conclusions, thus:

> It can be safely assumed that the ceramic tradition associated with the Salado occupation of the Cliff area of the Upper Gila did not develop out of local Mimbres Mogollon components or even out of the later Black Mountain phase of the eastern Mimbres. Instead, the Salado component of this site appears to ultimately reflect the migration of groups from areas to the west where Salado ceramic technologies first developed. . . . The initial production of early Salado poly-

chromes appears in the mountainous areas of central Arizona, and reflects the use of late Pueblo III Anasazi traditions from the Colorado Plateau as groups moved into the mountainous areas of Arizona. Another tradition resulting from such movements was even more directly influenced by the Tsegi Orange Ware tradition from the Kayenta-Tusayan region. This tradition was represented by the Maverick Mountain-Tucson polychrome group.

These observations on the Ormand Ruin ceramic assemblage seem entirely applicable to the Dutch Ruin and Villareal II assemblages.

Local Evolutions and Salado Continuity

Issues of local continuity and discontinuity plague the Mimbres area sequence with long-standing questions about the transitions from the Late Pit House period to the Mimbres phase (reviewed in Lekson 1999a), from the Mimbres to Animas (Black Mountain) phase (Creel 1999; LeBlanc and Nelson 1976; Nelson and LeBlanc 1986; Shafer 1999), and from the Animas (Black Mountain) to Cliff (Salado) phase. Hegmon and others (1999) split the late Mimbres horizon into two similar phases, "terminal" and "post-classic" Mimbres. The former refers to late Mimbres on multicomponent sites in the Mimbres valley and the latter refers to late Mimbres on single component sites in the Black Range, which may last a few decades longer than the Mimbres Valley "terminal" (Hegmon and others 1999). The wisdom of such fine divisions, based on excellent but as yet limited data, may be questionable. The same authors combine the plethora of similarly poorly known, prematurely defined post-Mimbres "phases" (early El Paso, Black Mountain, and Animas) into a single horizon, a terminological correction long sought and now welcomed (Lekson 1988, 1992a). In terms of local continuity and discontinuity from post-Mimbres to Salado, these authors extend Salado to include the Casas Grandes sites of southern Hidalgo County, New Mexico (Hegmon and others 1999, Fig. 5) and conclude that "continuity between Black Mountain and Cliff phases remains unresolved" (Hegmon and others 1999: 161).

Issues of continuity and discontinuity for the Mimbres and post-Mimbres phases in the Mimbres Valley and eastern Mimbres region, with "post-classic" Mimbres populations living in the hills through the thirteenth century (Nelson 1999) and "terminal" Mimbres populations in the Mimbres Valley itself (Creel 1999), and arguments for continuity (Creel 1999) and discontinuity (Shafer 1999) between Mimbres in whatever guise and the post-Mimbres Black Mountain phase, do not, apparently, apply to the Upper Gila region. Villareal II, the only excavated candidate for "Animas phase" status (comparable to the Black Mountain phase) has not survived critical reevaluation (see Chapter 3), and the few survey sites providing candidates for filling the "gap" between the Mimbres and Cliff phases are suspect. There appears to be a real hiatus of at least one and perhaps as much as two centuries between Mimbres and Salado.

The ceramic situation at Villareal II, with Mimbres Black-on-white sherds in every context that appears in initial analyses to be contemporary with later painted types (Lekson and Klinger 1973), may be a cautionary tale for "terminal" and "post-classic" Mimbres phases in the eastern Mimbres. But it is also possible that post-Mimbres prehistory in the western and eastern Mimbres took different trajectories.

Another complicating factor is the lack of controlled excavations at Woodrow Ruin (LA 2454), the "primate" Mimbres phase site in the Cliff Valley (Lekson 1990a). Few post-Mimbres sherds have been observed on the surface of this important site, but it is so much larger than any other pre-Salado site in the Cliff Valley that excavations at Woodrow could easily disprove any current reconstruction of Cliff Valley (and Upper Gila) prehistory. A similar situation obtains in the Redrock Valley, with the huge Redrock Cemetery Ruin (Lekson 1978a).

There seems to be little possibility of in situ local evolutionary development from Upper Gila Mimbres populations to Cliff phase Salado populations based on our current knowledge; that is, human populations did not adapt and evolve within the valleys of the Upper Gila region from one stage to the next. That development may have occurred *outside* the Upper Gila region, however: the local or regional development that constitutes the fourth model of Upper Gila Salado.

Local or Regional Developments and Salado Continuity

A recent and intriguing reconstruction of late pre-Contact history in southwestern New Mexico argues for continuity across a local region (Nelson and Anyon 1996). Nelson and Anyon's interpretation is admirably broad in scope (although, like Hegmon and others 1999, curiously truncated by modern state and international boundaries), arguing that populations moved from drainage to drainage in strategies of "short-term sedentism" leaving "fallow valleys" for future cycles of occupation. Fallow valleys were drainages occupied relatively briefly by sizable agricultural towns, and then left to regenerate and recover from intensive agriculture and depletion of wild resources, with "the option to aggregate and periodically move within a large open territory" (Nelson and Anyon 1996: 290; see also Nelson 2000: 323). Earlier, Nelson referred to this pattern as "short-term sedentism," suggesting that Mimbres Valley Salado populations were "in effect, wandering agriculturalists" (Nelson and LeBlanc 1986: 250). A similar mobility pattern is suggested for southeastern Arizona Animas phase villages (Douglas 1995). This proposed land-use system is a familiar one to archaeologists studying the Four Corners region, where it has a long history in the interpretation of Anasazi populations.

Nelson and Anyon's (1996) hypothesis is admirable for its scope and remarkable for its imagination, but difficult to evaluate in the near-absence of actual data accompanying their paper. Survey data compiled from the entire region do not support the fallow valley model prior to A.D. 1150 (Lekson 1992a; 1992c: 17). Those same survey data are far less useful for evaluating fallow valleys in the post-Mimbres period. Indeed, post-1150 cultural dynamics are universally acknowledged to be much less well understood than the earlier Pit House period and the Mimbres phase (Creel 1999; Hegmon and others 1999; LeBlanc 1980; Lekson 1992a; Nelson 1999; Nelson and Anyon 1996: 290; Shafer 1999).

Despite the difficulties of post-1150 chronology and cultural dynamics, Nelson and Anyon offer a detailed, decade-resolution, "postulated pattern of movement in the Late Pueblo Period" (Nelson and Anyon 1996, Fig. 3). They suggest initial movements of post-Mimbres populations from the Upper Gila and Mimbres valleys to the Playas Lake area, then back to the lower Mimbres, then to the Animas Valley, and finally north to the Upper Gila, with surplus Upper Gila Cliff phase populations recolonizing the Mimbres Valley in the small, short-term sites reported by Nelson and LeBlanc (1986).

Existing survey data are simply insufficient to assess this reconstruction (Lekson 1992a). Excavations in the Upper Gila, however, strongly contradict major parts of Nelson and Anyon's migrations, in particular the origins of Upper Gila Salado. Dean Wilson's conclusions about Ormand ceramics, quoted at length above, negate a key segment of the postulated pattern of movement: "Salado occupation of the Cliff area of the Upper Gila did not develop out of local Mimbres Mogollon components or even out of the later Black Mountain phase" (Wilson in Wallace 1998: 262). Dutch Ruin and Villareal II do not challenge Wilson's conclusion, and Dutch Ruin (in my opinion) strongly supports it.

Nelson and Anyon's model was a bold hypothesis set at a commendably large scale, and "short-term sedentism" may accurately describe the relatively small Salado occupation of the upper Mimbres Valley (the situation in the lower Mimbres Valley may have been rather different, as we shall see). Nelson and Anyon's model stayed well within the state and national boundaries of southwestern New Mexico, the conventionally accepted archaeological region, but ancient cultural dynamics, apparently did not.

Discontinuity with Puzzling Parallels

In summary, the Mogollon Highlands origin for Upper Gila Salado seems best supported by the ceramic data. "Southern" origins are negated by the redating of Paquime; in situ evolutionary schemes come to grief with the two-century gap between Mimbres and Salado in the Upper Gila; and the fallow-valleys model is contradicted by both survey and ceramic data. There remain, however, intriguing and possibly important similarities of detail between Upper Gila Salado and earlier Upper Gila and southwestern New Mexico phases. They include cimiento construction, burial practices, and some limited but striking parallels between Mimbres Black-on-white and Gila Polychrome.

Cimiento construction, with rows of upright cobbles forming the "footing stones" for thin puddled adobe walls, is not a Plateau or Mogollon Highlands technology (Cameron 1998). Sites with distinctive protruding cimiento stones are a hallmark of the northern Chihuahuan and northern Sonoran deserts. There are possible continuities with upright foundation stones in Mimbres phase sites such as Saige-McFarland (Lekson 1990a) and Swarts Ruin (Cosgrove and Cosgrove 1932). Mimbres foundation stones are generally two to three times larger than Salado cimientos, and Mimbres foundations may be related to the fact that the masonry walls were built above looser fill (for example, over filled pit structures), as this technique was only rarely used. Vertical stone footings appear to be rare in reported Black Mountain phase sites (Creel 1999; Ravesloot 1979), but cimientos are almost "typical" of Upper Gila and Mimbres Valley Salado construction (see Chapter 3; Nelson and LeBlanc 1986: 34–35; Wallace 1998: 78, 118).

Salado horizon burial practices are marked by their departure or difference from earlier burial practices in local areas. Woodson and others (1999: 77) note that across southeastern Arizona and southwestern New Mexico "the burial data demonstrate a consistent shift from flexed inhumation to cremation burial," whereas Salado in the Hohokam area is marked by precisely the opposite shift, from cremations to extended inhumation burials. Data from Dutch Ruin, Villareal II, and Ormand demonstrate a degree of variability, however: cremation cemeteries at Ormand, a mix of subfloor inhumations and cremations at Dutch Ruin, and a single inhumation at Villareal II. The contrast with earlier burial practices is perhaps less marked than might be expected. The Upper Gila has produced surprisingly few Mimbres phase or Late Pit House period burials, compared to the Mimbres Valley, but those burials show a range of practices: an elaborate Mangas phase burial at the Saige-McFarland site was an extended subfloor inhumation and later Mimbres phase burials included both subfloor inhumations and subfloor urn cremations (Lekson 1990a). Burial practices in the Mimbres Valley, thought typically to be subfloor flexed inhumations, are now revealed to encompass considerable variability, including primary and urn cremations in considerable numbers (Creel 1989; Shafer and Judkins 1996). Dutch Ruin appears to parallel the range of Mimbres practices, with subfloor urn cremations and inhumations with "killed" vessels of Gila Polychrome and other ceramic types. The Dutch Ruin burials are notable for their close parallels with earlier Mimbres practices (Chapter 2).

Several authors have noted striking similarities between Mimbres Black-on-white and Gila Polychrome (Crown 1994: 221–222; LeBlanc and Khalil 1976). Mimbres Black-on-white is conventionally dated from about A.D. 1000 to 1150; Nelson (1999) argues that it survives among relic populations into the early thirteenth century. Gila Polychrome is convincingly dated as no earlier than 1300, and it appears to be a solid fourteenth-century type. Thus, there is a hiatus of 150 years by conventional dating, narrowed to perhaps 75 years if we accept Nelson's dating of "post-classic" in the eastern Mimbres. How could graphic, visual artistic conventions survive those gaps? Visual arts may be expressed in various media, and it is possible that Mimbres artistic conventions were preserved in other forms, specifically in Jornada style rock art (Schaafsma 1992: 60–61). These are tenuous linkages between Mimbres and Salado, but the ceramic and artistic parallels are intriguing.

SALADO OF THE UPPER GILA

What do we know about the fourteenth century in southwestern New Mexico? Steven LeBlanc reviewed the period in 1980 (LeBlanc 1980) and I revisited it in a 1989 synthesis (Lekson 1992a). Compared to Mimbres archaeology, the immediately post-Mimbres period is notable for a dearth of publications and interest. But the last two years have seen an explosion of post-Mimbres studies, most notably: Margaret Nelson's *Mimbres in the Twelfth Century* (1999); Darrell Creel and Harry Shafer's contrasting views in *The Casas Grandes World* (C. Schaafsma and Riley 1999); and, most importantly, a remarkable group effort to untangle the "Scale and Time-Space Systematics in the Post-A.D. 1100 Mimbres Region" (Hegmon and others 1999). These publications give us subdivisions of Late, and Post-, and epi-Mimbres and interesting arguments about continuity between Mimbres and Black Mountain phases, but surprisingly little about the fourteenth century. The impression appears to be that *not much was going on* in the (post) Mimbres region during the fourteenth century.

That impression may well be true for the upper Mimbres Valley: Ben Nelson and Roger Anyon (1996) made the case that the Mimbres riverine settlements were "fallow valleys," building on Nelson and LeBlanc's (1986) *Short-term Sedentism*. This view of the fourteenth century, that only a few people were home, in rather bedraggled circumstances, was restated and reaffirmed in Nelson's (2000) summary remarks in the recent volume on the Salado (Dean 2000). Nelson thinks that fourteenth-century Salado sites in the Upper Mimbres valley were small and short-lived, part of a kind of trailer-park, valley-hopping settlement pattern. This may well be so, for the upper Mimbres Valley. But for the lower Mimbres Valley and, more importantly, the rest of the Mimbres region, the fourteenth century was extraordinary: huge towns with astonishing, cosmopolitan connections. The fourteenth century was perhaps the most dynamic, most spectacular archaeology of the Pueblo period in the Mimbres region. Remarkable things were happening in the fourteenth century, but one would never know that from the syntheses cited above, including my own. I tried to rectify this mistake in conference reports and book chapters (Lekson 1992b, 2000), but to no avail: a recent review of the "Gila Horizon" (*aka* Salado) omits entirely the Upper Gila and Mimbres areas (Crary and others 2001).

The fourteenth century was a time of remarkable developments in southwestern New Mexico and southeastern Arizona (Fig. 6.1). A full account of these dramatic

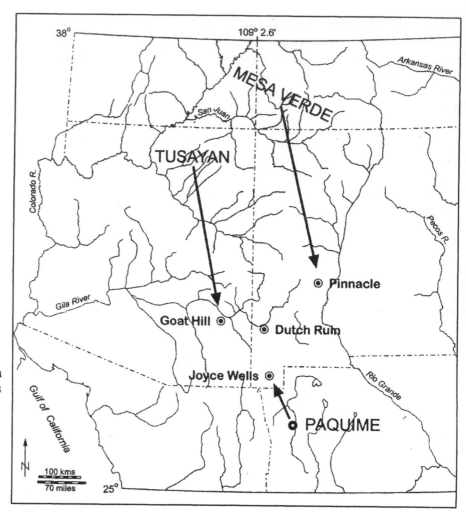

Figure 5.1. The fourteenth century in the northern Chihuahua desert and its northern neighbors.

developments is beyond the scope of this report, but they are briefly reviewed here insofar as they provide contexts for understanding the Salado of the Upper Gila. Around the edges of the old Mimbres region, new societies emerged as the result of local responses to long distance immigration. In the early fourteenth century, large Kayenta groups arrived in the Mogollon Uplands at settlements like Point of Pines (Haury 1958) and in Chihuahuan desert settlements like Goat Hill (Woodson 1999). At about the same time, large town-sized groups from the Mesa Verde area relocated to southwestern New Mexico in places like Pinnacle Ruin (Lekson and others 2001). The Casas Grandes valley, at the south end of the old Mimbres region, saw the astonishing rise of Paquime, which began between A.D. 1250 and 1300. The city of Paquime has been attributed to long-distance immigrations from Mexico (Di Peso 1974) or Chaco (Lekson 1999b) and, more conventionally, to local evolutionary processes (Whalen and Min-

nis 2001). Each of these developments marked three major cultural traditions that surrounded the Upper Gila: to the west, the interplay of Kayenta immigrants and local populations produced Salado; to the east, Mesa Verde migrants in at least three large towns are referred to as the Magdalena tradition; and to the south, Paquime was the center of the Casas Grandes world, which extended at least as far north as the settlement of Joyce Wells (Skibo and others 2002).

Mimbreños lived in the Upper Gila region in the eleventh and early twelfth centuries. Salado, Magdalena, and Casas Grandes were creatures of the fourteenth century. What happened in between? Not much, it seems, in the old Mimbres heartland (LeBlanc 1980) nor in the eastern Mimbres region (setting of the later Magdalena sites; Nelson 1999). In both areas, small populations appear to have reorganized into scattered hamlets, without large villages. Similarly, there is little evidence for late twelfth- and thirteenth-century occupations in the Upper Gila (Lekson 1990a, 1992a). A decade of survey and excavation has failed to find convincing evidence for large populations during this period in the southern Mimbres sphere (that is, northwestern Chihuahua), or, at least, that is my interpretation of Whalen and Minnis's data (2001). Thus, the future settings of Salado, Magdalena, and Casas Grandes were thinly occupied, if at all, in the late twelfth and thirteenth centuries.

The deserts between these three riverine areas (that is, the Lordsburg, Playas, and Animas valleys) have also been characterized as thinly settled or unoccupied during the late twelfth and thirteenth centuries (Hegmon and others 1999; Lekson 1992a; Nelson 1999). But in the fourteenth century, large villages in the lower Mimbres Valley and the Animas phase villages in the New Mexico "boot heel" appear in these previously empty spaces (Lekson 1992a; Skibo and others 2002). The boom of town-building in the deserts of southwestern New Mexico reflected, in some direct way, the remarkable developments around that area's margins: Salado to the northwest, Magdalena to the northeast, and Casas Grandes to the south.

Of Salado, Magdalena, and Casas Grandes, the last was clearly the most important development in the northern Chihuahuan desert during the fourteenth century. There is considerable debate on the origins of Paquime, the great central city of Casas Grandes (Di Peso 1974; Lekson 1999b; Minnis and Whalen 2001), but there can be little doubt that it was the largest and most cosmopolitan center of its time. It was a prodigious consumer of exotic materials such as Redrock serpentine.

The area encompassed by Salado, Magdalena, and Casas Grandes was then (and is now) remarkable for its minerals and mines: Redrock serpentine, possibly copper at Santa Rita, and turquoise at White Signal and, perhaps most importantly, at Hachita (Weigand and Harbottle 1993) were among the minerals mined during these late prehistoric centuries. Mining may well have begun during the Mimbres phase (Cosgrove and Cosgrove 1932: 62; McCluney 1968), but there is no reason to assume that the galleries and shafts observed by later explorers at Santa Rita, White Signal, and Hachita (Northrup 1944) were not fully developed during the thirteenth and fourteenth centuries. Considering Paquime's and Postclassic Mexico's demand for these minerals, it is highly likely that Paquime was actively engaged in mining and that the Upper Gila Salado were engaged at least in the mining of serpentine. The Magdalena settlements, even though located in mountains

famed for silver and gold, were not near sources of minerals mined by pre-Contact peoples.

Copper production at Paquime has been dismissed largely on typological grounds (Vargas 1995). Most, but not all, Paquime copper artifacts resemble west Mexican copper pieces. Typology, of course, could be a circular argument, if working knowledge and styles were imported. If west Mexican copper working was imported as an industry, Paquime artifact forms would indeed resemble west Mexican prototypes. Typological similarity has been argued to demonstrate transmission of copper technology, not just artifacts (Hosler 1994). Certainly the specialized technologies of raising macaws, and not just the birds, were imported to Paquime, and the same situation perhaps pertained to copper at Paquime. The key is metallurgy, as yet unstudied. Were west Mexican forms made with Chihuahuan ores?

Population shifts on enormous scales, from Kayenta to Salado, from Mesa Verde to Magdalena, and perhaps from the San Juan Basin to the Rio Casas Grandes framed the fourteenth-century colonization of the Upper Gila region. Ceramically, Tucson Polychrome (a southern variant of Kayenta pottery) was well represented at Dutch Ruin, as were the Chihuahua polychromes. A Mesa Verde-style mug in the Dutch Ruin collections may be out of context (Chapter 2); but if it indeed was associated with Dutch Ruin, that vegetal paint mug may have originated in the Magdalena settlements.

The ancient history of the Upper Gila region Salado must address issues much larger than subsistence, although that aspect of fourteenth-century life was fundamental. The conclusion that "the Ormand Village was self sufficient for all its subsistence and material needs" (Wallace 1998: 415) is an example of the deeply entrenched Southwestern aversion to large-scale regional dynamics. That provincialism, perhaps rooted in small "New Archaeology" spatial scales, preordains every settlement to unlikely self-sufficiency and every valley to impossible isolation. Larger scales and bigger thinking are indicated. Douglas (1995), Nelson (1999), and Nelson and Anyon (1996) provide examples of how this might be accomplished for the "area between" Salado, Magdalena, and Paquime. Their models may not be correct in every detail but they are models on appropriate scales, founded on useful and innovative concepts. Dutch Ruin and Villareal II provide another model, with the same probabilities for error and possibilities for insight.

The presence of ceramics from surrounding regions at Dutch Ruin and auxiliary information indicate there were connections between the Upper Gila Salado and a much larger world. But an equally important contribution of this site to our understanding of Upper Gila Salado is that the Dutch Ruin collections also demonstrate the usefulness of large avocational collections. Excavations on the scale of "Dutch" Fortenberry's and "Grandma" Bennett's work at Dutch Ruin will not be undertaken at any other large Upper Gila Salado sites in our lifetimes. Excavations on the scale of Villareal II, as limited as those were, are unlikely save through unforeseen CRM operations. Big questions do not always require big collections in our search for answers, but issues of large-scale regional dynamics are certainly easier to address with large collections like those from Dutch Ruin, Ormand, Dinwiddie, and Di Peso's remarkable, and never to be duplicated, excavations at Paquime. These thoughts underscore the tragedy of lost collections: those of Jack and Vera Mills from a half-dozen important sites, now unavailable and, even more heartbreaking, the apparent dispersal of Red and Virginia Ellison's collections from Kwilleylekia. To understand the Upper Gila Salado, Kwilleylekia was perhaps the key, irreplaceable site.

Another site, not yet mentioned here (and seldom mentioned in the literature), may be as important as Kwilleylekia to our understanding of post-Mimbres archaeology in southwestern New Mexico: the Black Mountain site (LA 49). This famous site, located on the Mimbres River near Deming, New Mexico, was visited by Walter Hough, Nels Nelson, and Alfred Vincent Kidder, but our best information comes from the Mimbres Foundation survey of 1974 (Minnis and LeBlanc 1979). That survey indicated at least five large adobe room blocks with a total of 300 rooms. Subsequent to that survey, the site was bladed and bulldozed. The Black Mountain site clearly postdates Mimbres, but surface ceramics support a dating to the Black Mountain phase, the Cliff phase, or both.

The Black Mountain phase, conventionally, represents the Mimbres Valley's post-Mimbres, pre-Salado period. The Black Mountain site was considered the "type site" of the phase. Curiously, this largest post-Mimbres site in the Mimbres Valley is ignored in the most-cited synthesis of Mimbres Valley population and settlement patterns (Blake and others 1986, in which their study area was truncated a short distance north of Black Mountain). Nor does it appear in recent synthe-

ses of post-Mimbres archaeology by Nelson (1999), Hegmon and others (1999), and Shafer (1999). Creel (1999) and Nelson and Anyon (1996) note the concentration of post-Mimbres population in the lower Mimbres Valley, but neither cite the Black Mountain site as a significant element of post-Mimbres settlement.

It seems hard to ignore a 300-room site. Even if it is completely destroyed, we have the 1974 survey records, which demonstrate with great clarity that the Black Mountain site was a major component (perhaps *the* major component) of post-Mimbres archaeology in the Mimbres Valley. Its 300 rooms make a difference. If the Black Mountain site indeed dates to the immediately post-Mimbres Black Mountain phase, then the Mimbres "collapse" collapses (Creel 1999; Lekson 1992b). Black Mountain and the other lower Mimbres Valley sites argue against a dramatic population drop and for a simple population shift (Lekson 1992b), although questions of cultural continuity or discontinuity remain (Creel 1999; Shafer 1999). If, on the other hand, the Black Mountain site is a later Salado era settlement, then the "short-term sedentism" model of Mimbres Salado (based on much smaller upper Mimbres Valley sites) requires serious review (Nelson and LeBlanc 1986). Even more intriguing, an occupation at Black Mountain that spanned both Black Mountain and Salado periods could support models of Salado origins in the Chihuahuan desert (LeBlanc and Nelson 1976), rejected here.

LeBlanc may be right about Salado; Nelson may be right; Wallace may be right; I may be right. The truth, we hope, is out there. But we will never resolve these issues without addressing the largest, most spectacular, and most difficult sites. Big questions often center on unique sites: Chaco and Paquime are two good examples (Di Peso 1974; Lekson 1999b). The Black Mountain site is badly damaged, but the site may still hold the key to several major questions of southern Pueblo archaeology: Mimbres to post-Mimbres continuity, the rise and role of Paquime, and even the origins of Salado. The Black Mountain site does not appear here as an afterthought or a postscript, but rather as a positive identification of where future research might focus if archaeologists are to resolve questions about post-Mimbres, Salado, and Chihuahuan archaeology in the southern Southwest.

The Villareal Sites

VILLAREAL I

The site of Villareal I was partially excavated by Harriet Cosgrove and C. Burton Cosgrove. Their field notes (Cosgrove and Cosgrove 1929: 4) indicate that a much larger ruin originally extended below the terrace (Fig. A.1) under agricultural fields that had "obliterated the upper wall courses" and all that remained was "a cluster of houses along the edge of a low bench...walls were of good rubble masonry, and ...no puddled adobe walls were encountered." They cleared four rooms, which contained "San Franciso Valley pottery" above an "early plaster on soil room" beneath the "pueblo rooms" in a stratigraphic situation similar to Villareal II. In a published summary, they concluded: "At the Villareal Ranch on the Gila River (Ruin 9 of the Museum Survey) Tularosa Black-on-white and corrugated wares were discovered in a stratigraphic position above Mimbres (Cosgrove and Cosgrove 1932: 111). Additional excavations by Fel Brunnett of the Chippewa Nature Center and the Upper Gila Project have not yet been published, but analyses are ongoing.

VILLAREAL III

Villareal III appeared to be a ten-room Mimbres structure, located on an isolated finger of the Gila Conglomerate bench (Figs. A.1, A.2). Operations at Villareal III consisted of a limited, grab-sample surface collection, mapping of the visible walls, and one 5-by-5-foot test pit.

Condition prior to excavation: Villareal III consisted of a low (3 feet tall) rubble mound. Some surface alignments of river cobbles clearly indicated walls. The central and eastern portions of the site had been disturbed. Surface artifacts were noticeably more dense just northwest of the room block, suggesting trash deposition in this area.

Sequence of excavation: Test Pit 1 was a 5-by-5-foot unit, placed against the presumed exterior of the western wall of the room block, in the area of heavy artifact concentration northwest of the site. This location was chosen to test the trash, expose a small portion of

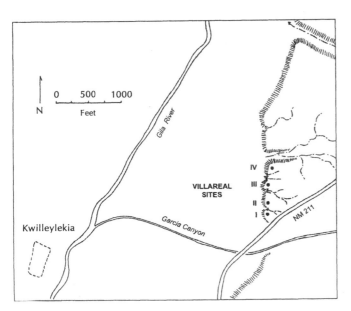

Figure A.1. Location of the Villareal sites in southwestern New Mexico (see Fig. 1.1).

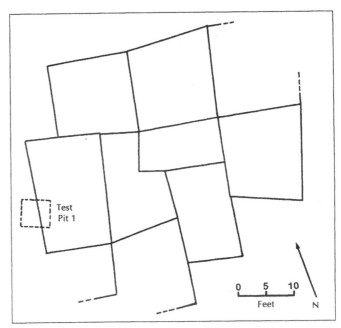

Figure A.2. Plan of visible walls at Villareal III, showing location of test pit.

wall, and test for architectural stratigraphy in this portion of the site. In fact, the test pit straddled the west wall it was intended to abut, and much of the wall was destroyed unwittingly during the excavation. This wall did not appear to be the exterior wall. Material was removed in arbitrary 6–inch levels, determined by a datum set at the northeast corner of the pit. Fill in the first three levels was fairly uniform, except for the partially deteriorated wall that ran through the center of the pit from north to south. The cobbles comprising this wall were removed, as it was thought that they represented rubble from a wall presumed to be at or near the east edge of the pit. At the base of Level 3, the true situation became apparent, and the real wall was defined. East of this wall a well-defined floor appeared at a depth of 17 inches, and to the west of the wall the floor of the test pit extended over a subfloor pit. A distinct floor level was defined in the west face of the test pit, at a depth equivalent to the floor east of the wall. However, the western floor did not extend very far into the test pit. The base of the subfloor pit was reached at a depth of 22 inches below datum. Fill was screened through ¼–inch mesh.

Fill: Fill above the floor level (Levels 1 through 3, surface to 17 inches below datum) was a homogeneous dark brown sand.

Floors: The floor east of the wall was a thin (approximately 1 inch thick) mud plaster applied directly on undisturbed soil. Floor west of the wall was observed only in the west face of the test pit. It appeared to be somewhat thicker, up to 1.5 inches thick, and rested on a cultural fill identical to that of the subfloor pit. The situation was not clear, but it appeared that the subfloor pit extended beyond the test pit to the north, west, and south (west of the wall) and that fill below the floor (west of the wall) was part of the fill of the subfloor pit.

Subfloor pit: The entire half of the test pit west of the wall appeared to be a subfloor pit, below a floor that was (in part) destroyed in excavation. This pit extended approximately 5 feet below floor level, and was defined only on its east edge, where the edge of the pit paralleled the foundation of the wall. Level 4 was limited to the contents of this pit. The most notable artifacts in the pit were a metate and two manos (GS 14, 15, and 16), which were on the floor of the pit against the east wall of the pit in the south end of the test pit. The long axis of the metate was parallel to the wall above it, and the metate was upside-down. The two manos were right side-up on the metate. The metate was not extensively used; however, the manos appeared to

be well worn. These kinds of items represent burial furniture, but no interment was noted in the area.

Wall: The wall running north and south through the test pit was defined just above its foundation, which consisted of a shallow (4 inch) trench filled with a tan adobe. Portions of the foundation were exposed in the east wall of the subfloor pit. Above this foundation, the wall appeared to consist of one and two widths of horizontally laid river cobbles that appeared to increase in size toward the base of the wall. At its base, the wall varied from 14 inches to 16 inches in width.

Ceramics and dating: Of the 294 sherds recovered from the test pit, 44 percent were Mimbres white wares. The classified painted and decorated sherds were predominately Mimbres Classic Black-on-white (66 sherds) with only 4 sherds of Mimbres Boldface Black-on-white. No earlier or later types were represented. The excavated portions of Villareal III appear to be Mimbres phase.

VILLAREAL IV

Villareal IV appeared to be a multicomponent site, with at least 9 pit house depressions and a room block (Fig. A.3) similar to, but slightly larger than, Villareal II. Surface material was limited to the area around the room block and the six westernmost depressions. There was scant material in and around the eastern three depressions. Operations were limited to a small grab-sample surface collection, mapping of the site, and a single 5–by–5–foot test pit.

Condition prior to excavation: The site appeared to be disturbed little, if at all. The room block consisted

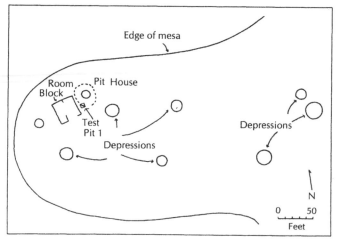

Figure A.3. Plan of Villareal IV in southwestern New Mexico, with depressions that may represent pit houses.

of a low (2-foot) mound with several exposed exterior wall stubs. It is possible that the block was "U" shaped with a small plaza enclosed on three sides, opening to the south. Wall stubs consisted of three rows of parallel, upright river cobbles, similar to the walls described above for the main room block at Villareal II. Pit houses were indicated by bowl shaped depressions, reaching a maximum depth of only about 2 feet below ground surface, surrounded by gravel rings. Surface artifacts were heaviest just to the east of the main room block, suggesting trash deposition in this area.

Sequence of excavation: Test Pit 1 was placed just east of the room block, on the southwest margin of a pit house depression. The excavation was intended to test what appeared to be a trash deposit and to establish the nature of the depression. The test was excavated in 5 arbitrary 6-inch levels, defined by a datum set on the southwest corner of the unit. Although the ground surface was relatively level in the area of the test pit, the extension of the gravel ring surrounding the pit house depression ran through the test pit from northwest to southeast. The southwest arc of the wall of a pit house was uncovered just east of the line of gravel on the sur-face of the pit. All material removed was screened through ¼-inch mesh hardware cloth.

Fill: Level 1 (surface to 6 inches) consisted of a fine powdery soil with few rocks. Levels 2 through 5 (6 inches to 28 inches) consisted of a dark brown, loose sand with a great many river cobbles.

Pit house: The edge of a pit house appeared about 15 inches below present ground surface; its wall sloped up to 45 degrees. The floor of the pit house was between 14 inches and 16 inches below the upper margin of the wall. There were no features and no evidence of plastering on the pit house wall or floor. The arc of the wall exposed in the pit and the configuration of the depression indicated a pit house up to 30 feet in diameter.

Ceramics and dating: A total of 497 sherds came from test excavations at Villareal IV. Painted and decorated pottery made up 21 percent of the collections. Identifiable decorated sherds were predominantly Mimbres Boldface and Mimbres Classic Black-on-white in equal proportions (28 sherds each), along with 7 sherds of Gila Polychrome. The ceramic assemblage indicated a multicomponent site extending from the Late Pit House period through the Mimbres and Cliff phases.

Lithic Material from Villareal II

Elizabeth Skinner (1974) and I analyzed the flaked stone items recovered from the investigations at Villareal II using a typology developed for the Upper Gila Project by James Fitting (1972b) and others. Collections from excavations totaled 2,008 pieces (Table B.1). Basic sorting categories were debitage, cores, flake tools, unifaces, bifaces, and combination tools (Fitting 1972b). Eight material types were defined for the Upper Gila Project lithic analyses: basalt, andesite, rhyolite, chert, chalcedony (various clear cherts), quartzite, agate (red or red-banded cherts), and obsidian. Considerably more information on the lithic items (measurements, weights, material details) is on file at the Laboratory of Anthropology in Santa Fe, New Mexico, and the University of Colorado in Boulder.

DEBITAGE

Debitage was the unmodified waste of lithic manufacture, which represented about 95 percent of the lithic material recovered. Sorting categories included blocky, flat, bifacial thinning flakes, and core rejuvenation flakes.

By far the most frequent categories of debitage were blocky and flat, which together made up all but 15 pieces of the debitage. The proportions of the two types were typically about 25 percent blocky to 75 percent flat flakes in all architectural units except Room 3, which had the smallest lithic assemblage of any room and a ratio of 40 percent blocky to 60 percent flat flakes. Ratios from combined floor fill and floor contexts were less uniform than the overall ratio of combined fills. The percentage ratios of blocky to flat flakes in floor fill and floor assemblages were lowest (about 15:85) in Rooms 1, 2, 4, and Pit House 1; highest (about 40:60) in Room 3 and Pit House 2; and intermediate (25:75) in Rooms 2 and 5.

Excavators recorded bifacial thinning flakes in the fill of Rooms 4 and 5, in the fill of Pit House 2, and in the floor fill contexts of Rooms 3 and 5. No bifacial thinning flakes appeared on floors. Very few (13) bifacial thinning flakes were recovered and no obvious concentrations were noted, nor did the occurrence of this kind of flake appear to correlate with high frequencies of flat flakes.

Only two core rejuvenation flakes were found, one each in the fill of Rooms 2 and 4. The distribution of undifferentiated debitage ("flakes") in surface collections is shown in Figure 3.8.

CORES

Cores were sorted into blocky, tabular bidirectional, biconvex, and plano-convex (or conical) types (Fig. B.1; Fitting 1972b). Of a total of 13 cores in the excavated sample, 8 were found in the general fill (in Rooms 3 and 4 and Pit Houses 1 and 2). The remaining 5 were in floor fill contexts: 2 in Room 1 and 3 in Room 2. No cores appeared on the floor of any room or pit house. Blocky cores and plano-convex cores were in fill and floor fill of rooms and in the fill contexts of both pit houses. Tabular bidirectional cores were encountered only in pit house fill contexts. Of the 9 cores excavated from room contexts, 7 were plano-convex. No biconvex cores were found in the excavations.

Cores from surface collections exhibited an interesting distribution. Of about 45 cores in the surface collections, half were recovered from the "northeast" concentration, one-fourth came from surface contexts in and around the room block, and one-fourth were scattered around the remainder of the bench surface (see Fig. 3.9). Blocky cores were equally distributed between the room block and the "northeast" concentration. Only two tabular cores were found in any surface context, and neither was near the room block (tabular cores from excavations were in pit house fill).

Plano-convex cores and biconvex cores also exhibited interesting distributions in surface collections: 12 plano-convex cores came from the "northeast" concentration; only 2 came from around the room block. Conversely, 6 biconvex cores were recovered near the room block, but only 3 were found elsewhere in the surface

Table B.1. Flaked Lithics from Villareal II

Lithics	Room 1			Room 2*			Room 3			Room 4			Room 5*
	Fill	Floor Fill	Floor	Fill	Floor Fill	Feature 9	Fill	Floor Fill	Floor	Fill	Floor fill	Floor	Fill
Blocky flakes	48	26	2	67	28	2	27	31	12	42	18		41
Flat flakes	214	144	16	197	129		40	62	4	132	107	2	180
Bifacial thinning flakes								2		1			2
Core rejuvenation flakes				1						1			
Blocky cores		1								1			
Tabular bidirectional cores													
Plano-convex cores		1			3		2			1			
Perforators		1			3					1			
Wedges									1				
Choppers	1												
Side-scrapers				2									
End-scrapers													
Concave scrapers				1									
Uniface perforators	1												
Chopping tools	1												
Knives	1			1							1		
Preforms								1		1		2	1
Biface perforators								1					1
Projectile points												1	
Combination tools	3	2					1						
Retouched-utilized flakes	4	3		9			8	4	2	4	4		5
Totals	273	178	18	278	163	2	78	102	18	184	130	5	230

Table B.1 (continued)

Lithics	Room 5*	Pit House 1			Pit House 2*		Feature 14	Unit A*			Unit B	Test Pit 1
	Floor Fill	Fill	Floor Fill	Floor	Fill	Floor fill		Fill 1	Floor Fill 1	Fill 2	Level 1	Level 1
Blocky flakes	10	9	14		22	14	7	4	3	1	1	19
Flat flakes	21	15	62	2	71	23	6	8		1	3	5
Bifacial thinning flakes	1				3				2	1	1	
Core rejuvenation flakes												
Blocky cores					1							
Tabular bidirectional cores		1			1							
Plano-convex cores					1							
Perforators												
Wedges						1						
Choppers												
Side-scrapers	1		1									
End-scrapers	1	1										
Concave scrapers		1										
Uniface perforators												
Chopping tools												
Knives		1										
Preforms	1				1	1						
Biface perforators												
Projectile points												
Combination tools												
Retouched-utilized flakes		1	2			1	1	1				1
Totals	35	28	79	2	100	40	14	13	5	3	5	25

* No lithics in Floor contexts of Rooms 2 and 5 and Pit House 2 or in Unit A Floor Fill 2.
NOTE: There were no biconvex cores in excavated deposits.

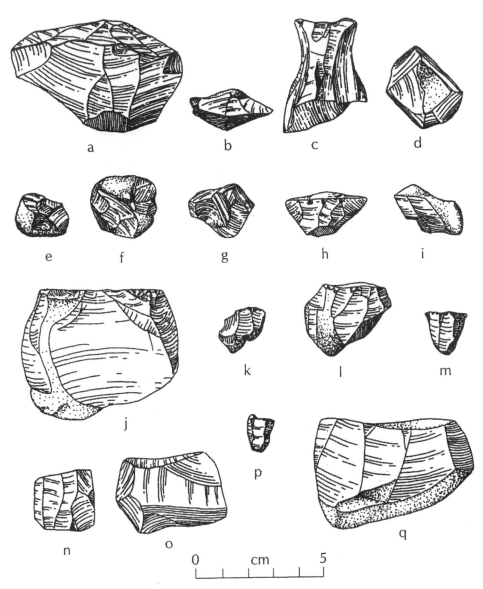

Figure B.1. Lithics from Villareal II: *a, b*, biconvex cores; *c–g*, blocky cores; *h–m, p, q*, plano-convex cores; *n, o*, tabular bidirectioncal cores.

collections. Most of the cores from excavated room contexts were plano-convex. If those excavated specimens were included in the spatial distribution, there probably would not be any significant distributional differences in core types between the room block area and the "northeast" concentration.

Chert was the most frequent material for cores of all types. Tabular cores were exclusively of chert. Plano-convex cores were of all materials (including the only core of quartzite). Biconvex cores were of all materials except quartzite and obsidian. Blocky cores included all materials except andesite and agate.

FLAKE TOOLS

Flake tools included retouched and utilized flakes, perforators, and wedges. In distribution the retouched and utilized flakes came from almost every context except the floor fill of Rooms 2 and 5 and the pit house fill contexts, but only two utilized flakes were found on a floor, in Room 3. These flakes were predominantly of fine grained materials, with about 70 percent of chert and approximately 20 percent of chalcedony, agate, and obsidian. The remaining 10 percent were almost exclusively of basalt, with a single utilized flake of andesite.

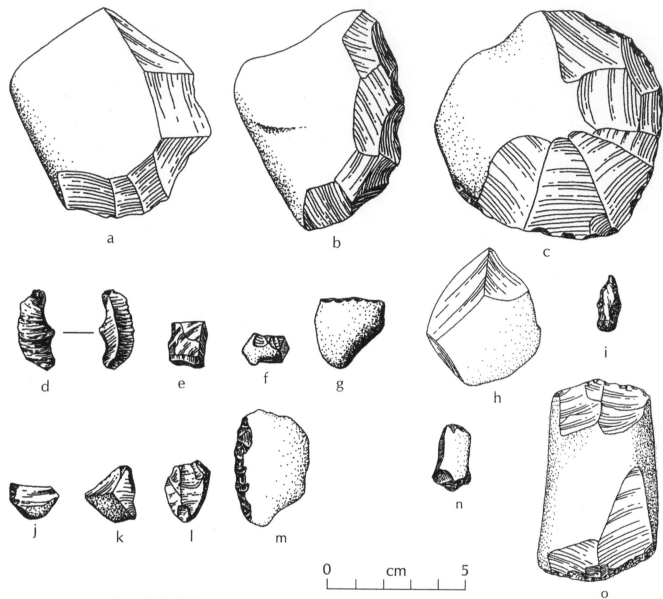

Figure B.2. Unifacial retouched tools from Villareal II: *a–c*, choppers; *d*, *e*, concave scrapers; *f*, *g*, end scrapers; *h*, *i*, perforators; *j–m*, side scrapers; *n*, *o*, wedges.

Unmodified perforators (projections on flakes) were in the fill of Room 4 and the floor fill of Rooms 1 and 2. Only 5 were found, and 3 perforators were from the floor fill of Room 2. The perforator from the floor fill of Room 1 (Fig. B.2*h*) was conspicuously larger than other perforators. Perforators on combination tools (below) were in the fill and floor fill of Room 1.

Wedges were rare, with only two coming from excavations (from floor fills of Room 3 and Pit House 2; Fig. B.2*n*, *o*). The marked differences between the two specimens from Villareal II suggest that this category perhaps included two different kinds of tools.

UNIFACES

Unifaces or unidirectionally retouched tools (Fitting 1972b) included choppers, side scrapers, end scrapers, concave scrapers, and unifacial perforators (Fig. B.2). Three choppers (Figure B.2*a–c*) were recovered, only one of which came from excavations (Room 1 fill). The single chopping tool (Fig. B.3*a*) in the excavations came from the same provenience. All the choppers were made on coarse grained materials like basalt, andesite, or rhyolite or from cobble or broken ground stone blanks.

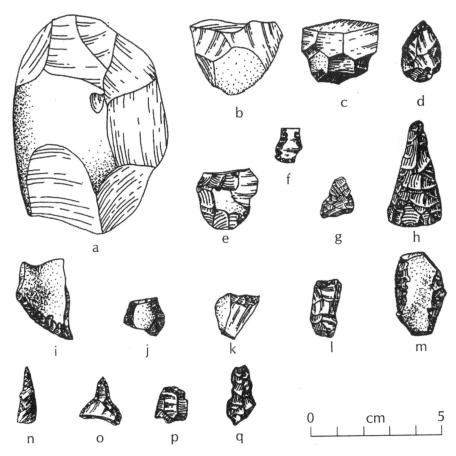

Figure B.3. Bifacial retouched tools from Villareal II: *a*, chopping tool; *b–h*, preforms; *i–m*, knives; *n–q*, perforators or drills.

Side scrapers (Figure B.2*j–m*) were in the fill of Room 2 and the floor fill of Room 5 and Pit House 1. Of 4 side scrapers, 2 were of obsidian and 2 were of chert. Side scrapers on combination tools were in the floor fill of Room 1 and the fill of Room 3.

End scrapers (Fig. B.2*f, g*) were rare, with only two specimens recovered in excavations. One was from the floor fill of Room 5 and one was from the fill of Pit House 1. Both were of fine grained materials. Concave scrapers (Fig. B.2*d, e*) were also rare, with only two specimens, both of obsidian. They were in the fill of Room 2 and Pit House 2. One unifacial perforator (Fig. B.2*h*) was in the floor fill of Room 1.

BIFACES

Bifaces and bidirectionally retouched tools (Fitting 1972b) included chopping tools, knives, preforms, bifacial perforators, and projectile points (Figs. B.3, B.4). Two chopping tools were recovered, one from the fill of Room 1 (Fig. B.3*a*) where the only excavated chopper was found and one from the "northeast" concentration. Both of these tools were of andesite.

Only six knives (five illustrated, Fig. B.3*i–m*) were recovered from Villareal II. They were made of chalcedony nodules and obsidian. Knives made on chalcedony nodules were found in the fill of Rooms 1 and 2, and the obsidian flake knives were in the floor fill of Room 4 and the fill of Pit House 1 and in surface collections from around the room block. Knives on combination tools (see Fig. B.4*i–o*) were made on obsidian and chert nodules and on chert flakes.

Preforms (Fig. B.3*b–h*) were relatively numerous, with nine from Villareal II. Preforms were in the fill of Rooms 4 and 5, in the floor fill of Rooms 3 and 5 and Pit House 2, and on the floor of Room 4. All preforms but one were made of fine grained materials: chert, chalcedony nodules, or obsidian.

Bifacial perforators or drills (Fig. B.3*n–q*) were less frequently encountered. Six were recovered from Villa-

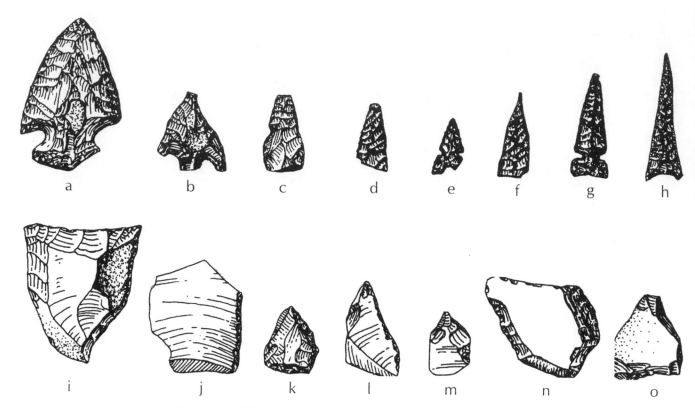

Figure B.4. Bifacial retouched tools, Villareal II: *a–h*, projectile points; *i–o*, "combination tools" (Fitting 1972b). (Full scale.)

real II, but only two came from excavated contexts: in the fill of Room 5 and the floor fill of Room 3. Four bifacial perforators were made on obsidian flakes, one on an obsidian nodule, and one on a chert flake.

Projectile points (Fig. B.4*a–h*) were common, with a total of eight specimens. Six were from surface contexts. Only one had a specific provenience within the room block, the floor of Room 4 (Fig. B.4*h*). It is a Late Pueblo period, slender, concave base, unnotched point. Most point fragments from the room block area were also Late Pueblo period styles, including three distal ends (Fig. B.4*c, d, f*) and two side-notched points (Fig. B.4*e, g*). These points are quite different from the several Pit House period broad style points, some basal notched, that were recovered from surface collections, including distal ends and one corner notched point (not illustrated). All other points were either fragmentary or unclassifiable. All points were of chert or obsidian.

COMBINATION TOOLS

Combination tools are best described by reference to Figure B.4*n–o*. There was a marked concentration of combination tools in the fill and floor fill of Room 1.

MATERIALS

The materials of flaked artifacts represented in the excavated assemblage included basalt (20%), andesite (11%), rhyolite (6%), chert (50%), chalcedony (5%), quartzite (1%), agate (2%), and obsidian (5%). The distribution of those materials is presented in Table B.2.

The "architectural unit" assemblages (combined fill, floor fill, and floors of rooms and pit houses) differed little from the general percentages listed. From floor fill and floor contexts only, however, there appeared to be slightly higher percentages of basalt tools and relatively lower percentages of chert tools in pit houses than in rooms. The frequencies of basalt and chert were about equal in the floor fill and floor of pit houses, and basalt was particularly frequent in Pit House 1. Room 3 stood out among room assemblages as having had a low percentage of chert artifacts and high percentages of basalt and rhyolite tools. With the exception of Room 3, the room fills and floors showed no marked variation from the overall site material percentages given above. Quartzite, particularly rare, was present only in Room 3.

Lithics from the systematic surface collection were categorized using a simpler, three-unit material classifi-

Table B.2. Distribution of Lithic Materials in Villareal II

Lithics	Room 1			Room 2*		Feature 9	Room 3			Room 4			Room 5*
	Fill	Floor Fill	Floor	Fill	Floor Fill		Fill	Floor Fill	Floor	Fill	Floor fill	Floor	Fill
Basalt	44	29	2	63	16	1	27	23	5	38	23	1	54
Andesite	40	29	2	26	15		5	14	2	10	16		18
Rhyolite	21	6	2	21	3		17	11	2	4	6		13
Chert	147	98	9	130	62	1	19	36	7	95	66	1	124
Chalcedony	12	4		21	13		5	8		13	5	2	9
Quartzite							3	5					
Agate	1	4	1	4	1		2	1		11	3		2
Obsidian	16	8	2	13	5			4	2	13	11	1	10
Totals	281	178	18	278	115	2	78	102	18	184	130	5	230

Table B.2 (continued)

Lithics	Room 5*	Pit House 1			Pit House 2*		Feature 14	Unit A*	Floor		Unit B	Test Pit 1
	Floor Fill	Fill	Floor Fill	Floor	Fill	Floor fill		Fill 1	Fill 1	Fill 2	Level 1	Level 1
Basalt	2	6	21	1	7	17	5	2	2		2	
Andesite		5	14		11	3	4	1				2
Rhyolite			2		3	6	3	1				2
Chert	21	13	30	1	69	11	1	5	3	3	2	12
Chalcedony	5		3		3	1		3				5
Quartzite					1							4
Agate	3	1	5		1						1	
Obsidian	4	3	4		5	2	1	1			2	
Totals	35	28	79	2	100	40	14	13	5	3	5	25

* No lithics in Floor contexts of Rooms 2 and 5 and Pit House 2 or in Unit A Floor Fill 2.

cation: coarse, fine, and obsidian. When the excavated lithics are combined into those three material classes, some striking differences appear between the excavated samples from rooms and pit houses and the materials represented in the surface scatter and the "northeast" surface concentration (Table B.3).

Considerable care was taken to completely collect surface units, so these differences probably do not reflect differential recovery between screened excavated samples and surface samples. Rather, the two distributions probably represent different activity sets, different temporal periods, or both.

Within tools and cores, unifacial and bifacial tools, preforms, and cores were disproportionately made of fine grained materials, particularly chalcedony and agate

Table B.3. Surface and Excavated Lithics from Villareal II by Material

Sample	Coarse	Fine	Obsidian
Surface	60	20	20
Excavated	35	60	5

compared to the total frequencies of these materials in the entire flaked stone collections. Compartively little basalt, andesite, or rhyolite was noted in tools and cores. A chi square test showed this pattern to be significant at the 0.01 level.

GROUND STONE

Ground stone artifacts consisted of manos, metates, and a single pestle (Figs. B.5–B.7, Table B.4). Almost all manos and metates were made of vesicular basalt. Manos (Figs. B.5a–j, B.6) were rectangular or "brick" shaped with single or double ground surfaces. Although the cross sections of Figure B.5b and e suggest it, none of the manos had finger grooves. Nearly all complete manos that were not part of architectural features came from the floor fill or were on the floor of Room 2. One complete mano (not in figure or table), was built into the west wall of Room 2 as one of the upright foundation stones or cimientos. One mano came from Pit House 2 fill.

No complete metates were recovered at Villareal II. One fragment (not illustrated) was built into the slab lining of a firepit (Feature 3). Two metate fragments (Fig. B.5o, m) were surface finds in the vicinity of the room block.

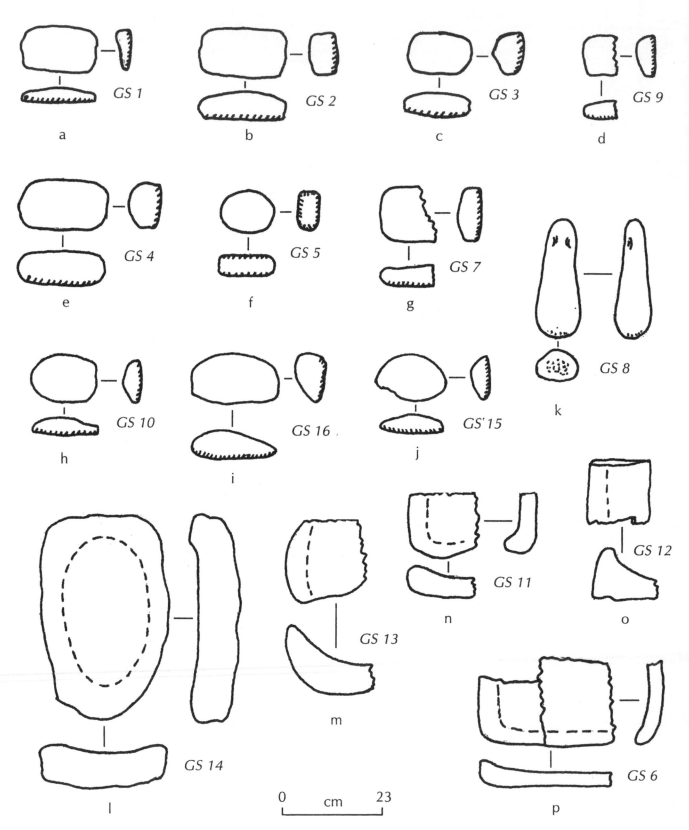

Figure B.5. Ground stone artifacts from Villareal II and Villareal III (see Table B.4): *a–j*, manos; *k*, pestle; *l*, metate; *m–p*, metate fragments.

Figure B.6. Manos from Villareal II.

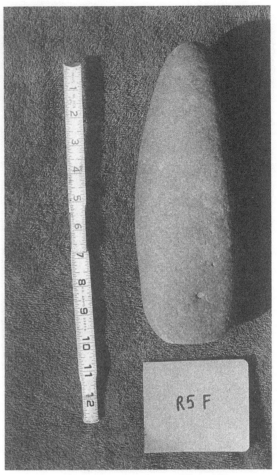

Figure B.7. Pestle from Villareal II.

Table B.4. Ground Stone from Villareal II and Villareal III

GS No.	Tool	Com-plete	Material	Provenience
Villareal II				
1	Mano	Yes	Vesic. basalt	Room 1, west wall
2	Mano	Yes	Sandstone or quartzite	Room 2, floor
3	Mano	Yes	Vesic. basalt	Room 2, floor fill
4	Mano	Yes	Vesic. vasalt	Room 2, floor fill
5	Mano	Yes	Vesic. basalt	Room 2, floor
6	Metate	No	Vesic. basalt	Feature 3, wall
7	Mano	No	Vesic. basalt	Room 3, fill
8	Pestle	Yes	Fine basalt or andesite	Room 5, floor
9	Mano	No	Sandstone	Room 5, floor
10	Mano	Yes	Vesic. basalt	Pit House 2, fill
11	Metate	No	Fine basalt or andesite	Pit House 2, fill
12	Metate	No	Vesic. basalt	Surface
13	Metate	No	Vesic. basalt	Surface
Villareal III				
14	Metate	Yes	Vasic. basalt	Test pit 1, level 4
15	Mano	Yes	Vesic. basalt	Test pit 1, level 4
16	Mano	Yes	Fine basalt or andesite	Test pit 1, level 4

Another metate fragment (Fig. B.5*n*) was in presumed wall rubble in the fill of Pit House 2. These few metate fragments appear to have come from roughly shaped, through trough forms.

A slightly modified river cobble (Figs. B.5*k*, B.7) from the floor of Room 5 may have been a pestle. Two small indentations pecked into its upper end perhaps represent finger grips. The lower end displayed extensive battering and crushing.

All other ground stone items were either fragmentary or were used as architectural elements. A metate (Fig. B.5*l*) and two manos (Fig. B.5*i* and *j*) were in close association in a subfloor pit at Villareal III.

References

Anyon, Roger, Patricia A. Gilman,
and Steven A. LeBlanc
  1981 A Reevaluation of the Mogollon-Mimbres Archaeological Sequence. *The Kiva* 46(4): 209–225.

Baker, Gayla S.
  1971 The Riverside Site, Grant County, New Mexico. *Southwestern New Mexico Research Reports* 5. Cleveland: Department of Anthropology, Case Western Reserve University.

Blake, Michael, Steven A. LeBlanc,
and Paul E. Minnis
  1986 Changing Settlement and Population in the Mimbres Valley, Southwest New Mexico. *Journal of Field Archaeology* 13: 439–464.

Breternitz, David A.
  1966 An Appraisal of Tree-Ring Dated Pottery in the Southwest. *Anthropological Papers of the University of Arizona* 10. Tucson: University of Arizona Press.

Brown, Jeffrey Lawrence
  1973 The Origin and Nature of Salado: Evidence from the Safford Valley, Arizona. MS, Doctoral dissertation, University of Arizona, Tucson.

Cameron, Catherine M.
  1998 Coursed Adobe Architecture, Style, and Social Boundaries in the American Southwest. In *The Archaeology of Social Boundaries*, edited by Miriam Stark, pp 183–207. Washington: Smithsonian Institution Press.

Chapman, Richard C., Cye W. Gossett,
and William J. Gossett
  1985 Class II Cultural Resource Survey, Upper Gila Water Supply Study, Central Arizona Project. Deuel and Associates, Albuquerque.

Clark, Jeffery J.
  2001 Tracking Prehistoric Migrations: Pueblo Settlers among the Tonto Basin Hohokam. *Anthropological Papers of the University of Arizona* 65. Tucson: University of Arizona Press.

Cosgrove, Hattie S., and C. Burton Cosgrove
  1929 Mimbres Valley Expedition, Field Notes, Season 1929, Gila Valley and Duck Creek. MS on file, Peabody Museum of American Archaeology and Ethnology, Harvard University, Cambridge.

  1932 The Swarts Ruin, A Typical Mimbres Site in Southwestern New Mexico. *Papers of the Peabody Museum of American Archaeology and Ethnology* 15(1). Cambridge: Harvard University.

Crary, Joseph S., Stephen Germick, and David E. Doyel
  2001 Exploring the Gila Horizon. *Kiva* 66(4): 407–445.

Creel, Darrell G.
  1989 A Primary Cremation at the NAN Ranch Ruin, with Comparative Data on Other Cremations in the Mimbres Area, New Mexico. *Journal of Field Archaeology* 16: 309–329.

  1999 The Black Mountain Phase in the Mimbres Area. In *The Casas Grandes World*, edited by Curtis R. Schaafsma and Carroll L. Riley, pp. 107–120. Salt Lake City: University of Utah Press.

Crown, Patricia L.
  1994 *Ceramics and Ideology: Salado Polychrome Pottery*. Albuquerque: University of New Mexico Press.

Dean, Jeffrey S., Editor
  2000 *Salado*. Amerind Foundation New World Studies Series. Albuquerque: University of New Mexico Press.

Dean, Jeffrey S., and John C. Ravesloot
  1993 The Chronology of Cultural Interaction in the Gran Chichimeca. In *Culture and Contact: Charles C. Di Peso's Gran Chichimeca*, edited by Anne I. Woosely and John C. Ravesloot, pp. 83–103. Albuquerque: University of New Mexico Press.

Di Peso, Charles C.
  1968 Casas Grandes and the Gran Chichimeca. *El Palacio* 75(4): 45–61.

  1974 Casas Grandes: A Fallen Trading Center of the Gran Chichimeca. Vol. 2, Medio Period. *Amerind Foundation Series* 9. Dragoon: Amerind Foundation.

  1976 Gila Polychrome in the Casas Grandes Region. In "The 1976 Salado Conference," edited by David E. Doyel and Emil W. Haury. *The Kiva* 42(1): 57–63.

Di Peso, Charles C., John B. Rinaldo, and Gloria J. Fenner
  1974a *Casas Grandes: A Fallen Trading Center of the Gran Chichimeca*. Vol. 8, Bone-Economy-Burials. Flagstaff: Northland Press.

Di Peso, C. C., J. B. Rinaldo, and G. J. Fenner (*continued*)
1974b   *Casas Grandes: A Fallen Trading Center of the Gran Chichimeca*. Vol. 6, Ceramics and Shell. Flagstaff: Northland Press.

Dittert, Alfred E., Jr., Editor
1966   The Cliff Highway Salvage Project. MS on file, Laboratory of Anthropology, Santa Fe, New Mexico.

Douglas, John E.
1995   Autonomy and Regional Systems in the Late Prehistoric Southern Southwest. *American Antiquity* 60(2): 240–257.

Doyel, David E., and Emil W. Haury, Editors
1976   The 1976 Salado Conference. *The Kiva* 42(1): 1–134.

Elson, Mark D., Miriam T. Stark, and David A. Gregory
2000   Tonto Basin Local Systems: Implications for Cultural Affiliation and Migration. In *Salado*, edited by Jeffrey S. Dean, pp. 167–191. Albuquerque: University of New Mexico Press.

Findley, James S., Arthur H. Harris,
Don E. Wilson, and Clyde Jones
1975   *Mammals of New Mexico*. Albuquerque: University of New Mexico Press.

Fish, Paul R., and Suzanne K. Fish
1994   Southwest and Northwest: Recent Research at the Juncture of the United States and Mexico. *Journal of Archaeological Research* 2(1): 3–44.

Fitting, James E.
1972a   Preliminary Notes on Cliff Valley Settlement Patterns. *The Artifact* 10(4): 15–30.
1972b   Chipped Stone from the 1967 Mimbres Area Survey. *Southwestern New Mexico Research Reports* 8. Cleveland: Case Western Reserve University.
1973   Four Archaeological Sites in the Big Burro Mountains of New Mexico. *COAS Monograph* 1. Las Cruces: COAS Publishing.

Fitting, James E., Claudia B. Hemphill, and Donald R. Abbe
1982   Class I Survey: Cultural Resources of the Upper Gila Water Supply Study Area. MS, Report prepared for the U.S. Bureau of Reclamation, Boulder City, Nevada. Springfield, Oregon: Hemphill Associates.

Fortenberry, Nanabell, and Gladys Bennett
1968   Potsherd Study at the Dutch Ruin. MS on file at the Museum of Northern Arizona, Flagstaff.

Gladwin, Harold S.
1957   *A History of the Ancient Southwest*. Portland, Maine: Bond Wheelwright.

Haury, Emil W.
1958   Evidence at Point of Pines for a Prehistoric Migration from Northern Arizona. In "Migrations in New World Culture History," edited by Raymond H. Thompson. *University of Arizona Bulletin* 29(2), *Social Science Bulletin* 27: 1–8.

Hayes, Alden C., Jon Nathan Young, and A. H. Warren
1981   Excavation of Mound 7, Gran Quivira National Monument, New Mexico. *Publications in Archaeology* 16. Washington: National Park Service.

Hegmon, Michelle, Margaret C. Nelson, Roger Anyon,
Darrell Creel, Steven A. LeBlanc, and Harry J. Shafer
1999   Scale and Time-Space Systematics in the Post-A.D. 1100 Mimbres Region of the North American Southwest. *Kiva* 65(2): 143-166.

Hoffmeister, D., and M. Lee
1963   Revision of the desert cottontail (*Sylvilagus audubonii*) in the Southwest. *Journal of Mammalogy* 44: 501–518.

Hosler, Dorothy
1994   *The Sounds and Color of Power: The Sacred Metallurgical Technology of Ancient West Mexico*. Cambridge: MIT Press.

Kessel, John L.
1971   Campaigning on the Upper Gila. *New Mexico Historical Review* 46(2): 133–160.

Kidder, Alfred Vincent
1962   *An Introduction to the Study of Southwestern Archaeology*. New Haven: Yale University Press.
[1924]

Kintigh, Keith
1996   The Cibola Region in the Post-Chacoan Era. In *The Prehistoric Pueblo World, A.D. 1150–1350*, edited by Michael A. Adler, pp. 131–144. Tucson: University of Arizona Press.

Klinger, Timothy C.
1975   Ceramics Represented in an Archaeological Survey of the Upper Gila Region of Southwestern New Mexico. MS on file, Laboratory of Anthropology, Santa Fe, New Mexico.

Lange, Richard C., and Stephen Germick, Editors
1992   Proceedings of the Second Salado Conference, Globe, AZ 1992. *Arizona Archaeological Society Occasional Paper* 24. Phoenix.

LeBlanc, Steven A.
1980   The Post-Mogollon Period in Southwestern New Mexico: The Animas/Black Mountain Phase and the Salado Period. In *An Archaeological Synthesis of South-Central and Southwestern New Mexico*, by Steven A. LeBlanc and Michael E. Whalen, pp. 271–316. Albuquerque: Office of Contract Archaeology, University of New Mexico.

LeBlanc, Steven A., and Carole L. Khalil
1976   Flare-rimmed Bowls: A Sub-type of Mimbres Classic Black-on-white. *The Kiva* 41(3–4): 289-298.

LeBlanc, Steven A., and Ben Nelson
1976   The Salado in Southwestern New Mexico. In "The 1976 Salado Conference," edited by David E. Doyel and Emil W. Haury. *The Kiva* 42(1): 71–79.

Lekson, Stephen H.

1978a Settlement Patterns in the Redrock Valley of the Gila River, New Mexico. MS, Master's thesis, Eastern New Mexico University, Portales.

1978b The Villareal Sites, Grant County, New Mexico. MS on file at the Laboratory of Anthropology, Santa Fe, New Mexico.

1982 Architecture and Settlement Plan in the Redrock Valley of the Gila River, Southwestern New Mexico. In *Mogollon Archaeology: Proceedings of the 1980 Mogollon Conference*, edited by Patrick H. Beckett, pp. 61–73. Ramona: Acoma Books.

1986 Mimbres Riverine Adaptations. In "Mogollon Variability," edited by Charlotte Benson and Steadman Upham. *University Museum Occasional Papers* 15: 181–189. Las Cruces: New Mexico State University.

1988 Regional Systematics in the Later Prehistory of Southern New Mexico. In *Fourth Jornada Mogollon Conference Collected Papers*, edited by Meliha S. Duran and Karl W. Laumbach, pp. 1–37. Tularosa: Human Systems Research.

1990a Mimbres Archaeology of the Upper Gila, New Mexico. *Anthropological Papers of the University of Arizona* 53. Tucson: University of Arizona Press.

1990b Sedentism and Aggregation in Anasazi Archaeology. In *Perspectives on Southwestern Prehistory*, edited by Paul E. Minnis and Charles L. Redman, pp. 333–340. Boulder: Westview Press.

1992a *Archaeological Overview of Southwestern New Mexico*. Las Cruces: Human Systems Research.

1992b Salado of the East. In "Proceedings of the Second Salado Conference, Globe, AZ 1992," edited by Richard C. Lange and Stephen Germick, pp. 17–21. *Arizona Archaeological Society Occasional Paper*. Phoenix.

1992c The Surface Archaeology of Southwestern New Mexico. *The Artifact* 30(3): 1–36.

1996a Southwestern New Mexico and Southeastern Arizona, A.D. 900 to 1300. In *The Prehistoric Pueblo World, A.D. 1150–1350*, edited by Michael A. Adler, pp. 170–176. Tucson: University of Arizona Press.

1996b Scale and Process in the Southwest. In "Interpreting Southwestern Diversity: Underlying Principles and Overarching Patterns," edited by Paul R. Fish and J. Jefferson Reid. *Anthropological Research Papers* 48: 81–86. Tempe: Arizona State University.

1999a Unit Pueblos and the Mimbres Problem. In "La Frontera: Papers in Honor of Patrick H. Beckett," edited by Meliha S. Duran and David T. Kirkpatrick. *Papers of the Archaeological Society of New Mexico* 25: 105–125. Albuquerque.

1999b *Chaco Meridian: Centers of Political Power in the Ancient Southwest*. Walnut Creek: Altamira.

2000 Salado in Chihuahua. In *Salado*, edited by Jeffrey S. Dean, pp. 275–294. Amerind Foundation New World Studies Series. Albuquerque: University of New Mexico Press.

Lekson, Stephen H., and Timothy C. Klinger

1973 Villareal II: Preliminary Notes on an Animas Phase Site in Southwestern New Mexico. *Awanyu* 1(2): 33–38.

Lekson, Stephen H., Karl Laumbach, Curtis Nepstad-Thornberry, Brian Yunker, Toni Laumbach, David Cain, David Hill, and Jim Wakeman

2001 Preliminary Report on the 2000 Research Season, Featuring Excavations at the Pinnacle Ruin, Cañada Alamos, New Mexico. *Human Systems Research Report* 2011. Las Cruces: Human Systems Research.

Lindsay, Alexander J., Jr.

1992 Tucson Polychrome: History, Dating, Distribution, and Design. In "Proceedings of the Second Salado Conference, Globe, AZ 1992," edited by Richard C. Lange and Stephen Germick, pp. 230–237. *Arizona Archaeological Society Occasional Paper*. Phoenix.

Lindsay, Alexander J., Jr., and Calvin H. Jennings

1968 Salado Red Ware Conference, Ninth Southwestern Ceramic Seminar, October 13–14, 1967. *Ceramic Series* 4. Flagstaff: Museum of Northern Arizona.

McCluney, Eugene B.

1968 A Mimbres Shrine at the West Baker Site. *Archaeology* 21(3): 196–205.

McKenna, Peter J., and James E. Bradford

1989 TJ Ruin, Gila Cliff Dwellings National Monument, New Mexico. *Southwest Cultural Resources Center Professional Paper* 21. Santa Fe: National Park Service.

Mills, Jack P., and Vera M. Mills

1972 The Dinwiddie Site: A Prehistoric Salado Ruin on Duck Creek, Western New Mexico. *The Artifact* 10(2): 1–50.

1978 The Curtis Site: A Prehistoric Village in the Safford Valley. Privately printed, Elfrida, Arizona.

Minnis, Paul E., and Steven A. LeBlanc

1979 The Destruction of Three Sites in Southwestern New Mexico. In "Vandalism of Cultural Resources: The Growing Threat to Our Nation's Heritage," edited by Dee F. Green and Steven LeBlanc. *Cultural Resources Report* 28: 69–78. Albuquerque: USDA Forest Service.

Moore, Mrs. Glen E., and Mrs. Joe Ben Wheat

1951 An Archaeological Cache from Hueco Basin, Texas. *Bulletin of the Texas Archaeological and Paleontological Society* 22: 144–163.

Nelson, Ben A.
2000   Salado at the End of the Twentieth Century. In *Salado*, edited by Jeffrey S. Dean, pp. 321–326. Amerind Foundation New World Studies Series. Albuquerque: University of New Mexico Press.

Nelson, Ben A., and Roger Anyon
1996   Fallow Valleys: Asynchronous Occupations in Southwestern New Mexico. *Kiva* 61(3): 275–294.

Nelson, Ben A., and Steven A. LeBlanc
1986   *Short-term Sedentism in the American Southwest: The Mimbres Valley Salado*. Albuquerque: University of New Mexico Press.

Nelson, Margaret C.
1999   *Mimbres during the Twelfth Century: Abandonment, Continuity, and Reorganization*. Tucson: University of Arizona Press.

Northrup, Stuart Alvord
1944   *Minerals of New Mexico*. Albuquerque: University of New Mexico Press.

Ravesloot, John C.
1979   The Animas Phase: The Post-Classic Mimbres Occupation of the Mimbres Valley, New Mexico. MS, Master's thesis, Department of Anthropology, Southern Illinois University, Carbondale.

Reid, J. Jefferson
1989   A Grasshopper Perspective on the Mogollon of the Arizona Mountains. In *Dynamics of Southwest Prehistory*, edited by Linda S. Cordell and George J. Gumerman, pp. 65–97. Washington: Smithsonian Institution Press.

Reid, J. Jefferson, and Stephanie Whittlesey
1997   *The Archaeology of Arizona*. Tucson: University of Arizona Press.

Robinson, William J., and Catherine M. Cameron
1991   *A Directory of Tree-Ring Dated Prehistoric Sites in the American Southwest*. Tucson: Laboratory of Tree-Ring Research, University of Arizona.

Schaafsma, Curtis R., and Carroll L. Riley, Editors
1999   *The Casas Grandes World*. Salt Lake City: University of Utah Press.

Schaafsma, Polly
1992   *Rock Art of New Mexico*. Santa Fe: Museum of New Mexico Press.

Schroeder, K. J.
1992   Mortuary Analysis of a Small Salado Cemetery Near Safford, Arizona. In "Proceedings of the Second Salado Conference, Globe, AZ 1992," edited by Richard C. Lange and Stephen Germick, pp. 201–205. *Arizona Archaeological Society Occasional Paper*. Phoenix.

Shafer, Harry J.
1999   The Mimbres Classic and Postclassic: A Case for Discontinuity. In *The Casas Grandes World*, edited by Curtis R. Schaafsma and Carroll L.

Riley, pp. 121–133. Salt Lake City: University of Utah Press.

Shafer, Harry J., and Constance K. Judkins
1996   Archaeology at the NAN Ruin, 1996 Season. *The Artifact* 34(3–4): 1–67.

Skibo, James M., Eugene B. McCluney, and William H. Walker
2002   *The Joyce Wells Site: On the Frontier of the Casas Grandes World*. Salt Lake City: University of Utah Press.

Skinner, Elizabeth
1974   Similarity of Lithic Industries in the Burro Mountains and the Cliff Valley of Southwestern New Mexico. *The Artifact* 12(3): 26–44.

Tyberg, Joel Jay
2000   Influences, Occupation, and Salado Development at the Solomonsville Site. MS, Master's thesis, University of Colorado, Boulder.

Vargas, Victoria D.
1995   Copper Bell Trade Patterns in the Prehispanic U.S. Southwest and Northwest Mexico. *Arizona State Museum Archaeological Series* 187. Tucson: University of Arizona.

Wallace, Laurel T.
1998   The Ormand Village: Final Report on the 1965–1966 Excavation. *Archaeology Notes* 229. Santa Fe: Office of Archaeological Studies, Museum of New Mexico.

Weigand, Phil C., and Garman Harbottle
1993   The Role of Turquoise in the Ancient Mesoamerican Trade Structure. In *The American Southwest and Mesoamerica: Systems of Prehistoric Exchange*, edited by Jonathon E. Ericson and Timothy G. Baugh, pp 159–177. New York: Plenum Press.

Whalen, Michael E.
1985   Chronological Studies in the Jornada Area. In *Views of the Jornada Mogollon: Proceedings of the Second Jornada Mogollon Archaeology Conference*, edited by Patrick H. Beckett and Regge N. Wiseman, pp 345–358. Santa Fe: New Mexico Historical Preservation Division.

Whalen, Michael E., and Paul E. Minnis
2001   *Casas Grandes and Its Hinterland: Prehistoric Regional Organization in Northwest Mexico*. Tucson: University of Arizona Press.

Wilson, C. Dean
1998   Ormand Ceramic Analysis. In "The Ormand Village: Final Report on the 1965–1966 Excavation," by Laurel T. Wallace. *Archaeology Notes* 229: 195–285. Santa Fe: Office of Archaeological Studies, Museum of New Mexico.

Wiseman, Regge N.
1981   Playas Incised, Sierra Blanca Variety: A New Pottery Type in the Jornada Mogollon. In *Trans-*

actions of the 16th Regional Archaeological Symposium for Southeastern New Mexico and Western Texas, pp. 21–27. Midland: Midland Archaeological Society.

Woodson, Michael Kyle
1999   Migrations in Late Anasazi Prehistory: The Evidence from the Goat Hill Site. *Kiva* 65(1): 63–84.

Woodson, M. Kyle, Thomas E. Jones, and Joseph S. Crary
1999   Exploring Late-Prehistoric Mortuary Patterns of Southeastern Arizona and Southwestern New Mexico. In *Sixty Years of Mogollon Archaeology*, edited by Stephanie M. Whittlesey, pp 67–79. Tucson: SRI Press.

Woosely, Anne I., and Allan J. McIntyre
1996   *Mimbres Mogollon Archaeology: Charles C. Di Peso's Excavations at Wind Mountain*. Albuquerque: University of New Mexico Press.

Woosely, Anne I., and Bart Olinger
1993   The Casas Grandes Ceramic Tradition: Production and Exchange of Ramos Polychrome. In *Culture and Contact: Charles C. Di Peso's Gran Chichimeca*, edited by Anne I. Woosely and John C. Ravesloot, pp 105–131. Albuquerque: University of New Mexico Press.

Woosely, Anne I., and John C. Ravesloot, Editors
1993   *Culture and Contact: Charles C. Di Peso's Gran Chichimeca*. Albuquerque: University of New Mexico Press.

Index

Abstract

Salado refers to a broad geographic distribution in the southern Southwest of several types of polychrome pottery. In some areas, this pottery appears to be a "veneer" over or in addition to existing, local ceramic traditions. In other areas, large sites with Salado pottery appear in districts then lacking substantial populations. Two sites in the Upper Gila River valley in southwestern New Mexico provide new insight on Salado.

The Villareal II site was a five-room farmstead; the Dutch Ruin site was a 150-room pueblo. These two sites represent the extremes of Salado settlement patterns in the Upper Gila area. Both sites were excavated in the early to mid 1970s. Villareal II was systematically excavated by professional archaeologists, and Dutch Ruin was partially excavated by avocational archaeologists. Collections vary accordingly: the Villareal II collections consist almost exclusively of sherds and lithics and the Dutch Ruin collections include about sixty whole or reconstructed ceramic vessels, finished tools, jewelry, and little else. By combining these disparate sets of information, an interesting picture of Salado settlements emerges.

Analyses of these two sites and data from several other Upper Gila Salado sites suggest a fourteenth-century Salado migration into an area with negligible population immediately preceding that event. Throughout the fourteenth century, Salado communities in the Upper Gila were integrated into the larger Salado horizon and closely connected to Casas Grandes, as indicated by the export of serpentine ricolite to the city of Paquime. Villareal II was one of several small farmsteads surrounding much larger Salado towns, such as Dutch Ruin. Large towns had extensive middens, numerous burials, and evidence of remodeling and reconstruction that indicated long-term sedentism. Salado in the Upper Gila region appears to be a substantial in-migration of Mogollon Upland populations into what was a vacant river valley.

Resumen

En el suroeste norteamericano, Salado se refiere a una amplia distribución geográfica de varios tipos de cerámica polícroma. En algunas áreas, esta cerámica aparece junto a otras tradiciones cerámicas locales. En otras áreas, sitios grandes con cerámica Salado aparecen en distritos de baja población. Dos sitios en el alto valle del Río Gila al suroeste de Nuevo México proveen nueva información sobre el fenómeno Salado.

El sitio Villareal II fue un rancho de cinco habitaciones; el sitio Dutch fue un pueblo de 150 habitaciones. Estos dos sitios representan extremos en el patrón de asentamiento Salado en el alto Gila. Ambos sitios fueron excavados en la década de 1970. Villareal II fue sistematicamente excavado por arqueólogos profesionales, mientras que el sitio Dutch fue excavado parcialmente por aficionados. Las colecciones, por lo tanto, son distintas: la colección de Villareal II consiste casi completamente de tiestos y lítica mientras que la colección de Dutch incluye cerca de sesenta vasijas completas y reconstruibles, herramientas acabadas, joyería, y casi nada más. Al combinar estos dos conjuntos de datos se obtiene una imagen interesante sobre los asentamientos Salado.

El análisis de estos dos sitios y los datos de algunos otros sitios Salado en el alto Gila sugieren que los inmigrantes Salado del siglo catorce arribaron a un área previamente poblada por muy poca gente. A través del siglo catorce, las comunidades Salado del alto Gila fueron integradas en el más amplio horizonte Salado y se conectaron muy cercamente con Casas Grandes, como lo indica la exportación de serpentina ricolita a la ciudad de Paquimé. Villareal II fue uno de aquellos ranchos que rodearon sitios Salado mucho más grandes, tales como el sitio Dutch. Los pueblos grandes tuvieron basurales extensos, numerosos enterramientos y evidencia de remodelamiento y reconstrucción que indican sedentismo prolongado. El fenómeno Salado en la región del alto Gila parece haber resultado de una inmigración substancial de poblaciones provenientes de la sierra Mogollón a un valle previamente vacante.

ANTHROPOLOGICAL PAPERS OF THE UNIVERSITY OF ARIZONA

Anthropological Papers listed as O.P., D are available as Docutech reproductions (high quality xerox) printed on demand. They are tape or spiral bound and nonreturnable.